13.99
D0276584
The South East Essex
College of Arts & Technology
30130504033850
O/R
8/96
STL
362.4
FOR
C/R

# Special Parents

**Open University Press**
Children With Special Needs Series

Editors

PHILLIP WILLIAMS
*Emeritus Professor of Education*
*University College of North Wales, Bangor.*

PETER YOUNG
*Formerly Tutor in the education of children with learning difficulties, Cambridge Institute of Education; educational writer, researcher and consultant.*

This is a series of short and authoritative introductions for parents, teachers, professionals and anyone concerned with children with special needs. The series will cover the range of physical, sensory, mental, emotional and behavioural difficulties, and the changing needs from infancy to adult life in the family, at school and in society. The authors have been selected for their wide experience and close professional involvement in their particular fields. All have written penetrating and practical books readily accessible to non-specialists.

TITLES IN THE SERIES

**Changing Special Education**
*Wilfred K. Brennan*
**Curriculum for Special Needs**
*Wilfred K. Brennan*
**The Early Years**
*Maurice Chazan and Alice Laing*
**Residential Special Education**
*Ted Cole*
**Working With Parents**
*Cliff Cunningham and Hilton Davis*
**Understanding Learning Difficulties**
*Kathleen Devereux*
**Special Education: The Way Ahead**
*John Fish*
**Special Parents**
*Barbara Furneaux*
**Deaf-Blind Infants and Children**
*J.M. McInnes and J.A. Treffry*
**Educating Hearing-Impaired Children**
*Michael Reed*
**Helping the Maladjusted Child**
*Dennis Stott*
**The Teacher is the Key**
*Kenneth Weber*
**How to Reach the Hard to Teach**
*Paul Widlake*
**Special Education in Minority Communities**
*Phillip Williams (ed.)*
**Dyslexia or Illiteracy?**
*Peter Young and Colin Tyre*

In preparation

**Beyond Childhood**
*Robin Jackson*
**Educating the Gifted Child**
*Joan Freeman*

# Special Parents

**Barbara Furneaux**

Open University Press
*Milton Keynes · Philadelphia*

Open University Press
Open University Educational Enterprises Limited
12 Cofferidge Close
Stony Stratford
Milton Keynes MK11 1BY

and
242 Cherry Street
Philadelphia, PA 19106, USA

First published 1988



*British Library Cataloguing in Publication Data*

Furneaux, Barbara
Special parents.—(Children with special needs).
1. Parents of handicapped children
I. Title II. Series
362.4'088054

ISBN 0-335-15123-X
ISBN 0-335-15122-1 Pbk

*Library of Congress Cataloging in Publication Data*

Furneaux, Barbara.
Special parents.
(Children with special needs series)
1. Parents of handicapped children. I. Title. II. Series.
HQ759.913.F87 1988
306.8'74—dc19 88-36877

ISBN 0 335 15123 X
ISBN 0 335 15122 1 Pbk

Typeset by Colset (Pte) Ltd
Printed in Great Britain by St Edmundsbury Press, Bury St Edmunds

# Contents

# Acknowledgements

I have been helped in the preparation of this book by many people who have generously given their time and shared their knowledge and experiences. To all of them I offer my sincere gratitude.

First mention must go to the many parents who have contributed. Many of them did not always find it easy to speak as freely as they did of their experiences, but they did so hoping that, by sharing them in this way, life will be made easier in consequence for all the parents of children with special needs in the future.

My thanks are due also to all the professionals who have helped, the doctors, teachers, nurses, psychologists, health visitors, social workers and research workers.

My particular thanks are due to the following,

Mrs Barbara Crowe, Southend and District Society for Mentally Handicapped Children.
Mrs Carol M. Myer, until recently principal of White Lodge Centre.
Sister Gascoigne and the staff at Honeylands, Exeter.
Paul Ennals, head of welfare services at SENSE.
Mrs Angela Simmons, social worker, Borough of Elmbridge.
Julian Kramer, Derbyshire Education Authority.
Dr M. V. Hope, senior medical officer, East Surrey.
Mrs Geraldine Williams and Mrs Maria Evans, Surrey County Council.
Mr Jim Hall, Church of England Children's Society.
And finally to all those who allowed me to visit their various establishments.

# Series Editors' Introduction

Children with special needs make special demands on their parents. This is the theme of Barbara Furneaux's book. In it she discusses the nature of those demands, the stresses to which they give rise and illustrates ways in which the parents have found relief. Her writing is based on her experiences as the Head of a special school, on impressions gained from visiting a variety of organisations and on opinions obtained from an informal questionnaire enquiry.

But she has not written an academic treatise. Her material offers an easy-to-read and at times moving and sensitive account of the feelings and emotions of parents. This is perhaps most evident where the parents are allowed to speak for themselves: there are few readers who will not sympathise with them over the insensitivity and thoughtlessness that they have met and which is so poignantly revealed in their brief comments. The early chapters, dealing with the ways in which parents learn of and react to their child's handicap, illustrate clearly the need for greater understanding on the part of the services involved. But all is not gloom: there are illustrations of good practice as well as bad. Indeed one of the many strengths of the book is that throughout its pages the author is at pains to offer examples of procedures, practices and organisations – from both the public and the voluntary sector – that parents have found supportive and helpful.

Concern about parents is not new. 'Parents as Partners' is a slogan that has led to far greater involvement of parents in the education of children with special needs. 'Integration' has resulted in some seriously-handicapped children who previously might have been educated in residential schools now attending their neighbourhood school and living at home. 'Community Care' has had a similar effect – some seriously-handicapped children living at home instead of in hospital. These developments have been sought by many parents and welcomed by them, for they represent policies which offer the children a more natural and richer childhood. But they are policies which make extra demands on parents, demands on their time, on their energies, on their patience, on their affection – sometimes to a degree which is quite beyond the ken of most of us. This touches on the issue that 'Special Parents' raises most sharply.

'. . . the right to work, to go to cinemas, to enjoy outdoor sport, to have a family life and a social life and a love life, to contribute materially to the community, to have the usual choices of association, movement and activity, to go on holiday to the usual places . . .'[1] – these words appear in the report of the Snowdon Working Party. They refer to rights claimed for the physically disabled. After reading 'Special Parents' we are forced to ask if this claim should not be made with equal force for the parents of some children with serious special needs. In our concern to integrate the children are we in danger of forgetting that their parents need integration too? Should not some of those examples of helpful practice (e.g. respite care) that the book describes be far more widely available?

The book moves on from the issues raised by the early years and by schooling to examine the opportunities offered to the children after school. Again, school-leaving is a transition that all parents face, but again it raises special problems for the parents of children with special needs. Once again the book outlines some of the solutions that parents have found helpful.

It is not always easy for parents to express their feelings when meeting the experts and it is a tribute to the author that she has succeeded in eliciting them so clearly. This is a book that begins and ends with the authentic voice of the parent. It is a voice that deserves to be heard, not least by the professionals to whom the parents turn for information, for guidance, and perhaps most of all, for understanding.

Phillip Williams
Peter Young

1. Integrating the Disabled. Report of the Snowdon Working Party, 1976, quoted on p. 99, Department of Education and Science, 1978, Children with Special Needs, London, H.M.S.O. (Warnock Report).

# Introduction

One of the major improvements in the educational field in the last few years has been the growth of interest in the needs of the handicapped child. Progress has been rapid. Until 1971, when the Education (Handicapped Children) Act became law, the severely mentally handicapped were excluded from the educational system altogether; now, as a matter of policy, serious plans are being made to integrate as many handicapped children as possible into the normal schools. In consequence of this the parents of such children no longer have to cope with the knowledge and, in the eyes of many, the stigma, both of learning that their child had been labelled as 'unsuitable for normal education' and of the feeling of being a social outcast that this brought to many of them. But what of the other needs of the parents – needs both practical, emotional and social? Is too much emphasis being placed on the needs of the children and too little on the needs of the parents? The answer to the first part of this question must surely be 'no'. Nevertheless it does seem that with regard to the second part a further question should be asked and that is, 'Are the parents expected to pay too high a price to meet the needs of their children? Do we, the community, do all that we should to help them in their unsought dilemma?'

This question first became of great importance to me in the course of one of the regular parent-group meetings we used to hold at the school of which I was then headteacher. The meeting had been proceeding in its usual friendly co-operative way, with the parents discussing their children and exchanging information on the ways they coped with the problems they experienced. One of the mothers, who until then had been a quiet but friendly member of the group, suddenly said, 'I was just remembering the day when I heard the truth about Luke.' Luke was the younger of her two children, both of whom were handicapped, although in different ways. The meeting came to a sudden hush as we all stopped talking and looked expectantly towards her. Then, very simply but very movingly, she told her story. Her marriage had been adversely affected when her first handicapped child had been born, but when four years later she had her second child who in his first year appeared to be normal she felt full of hope for the future. Gradually however her fears grew that this child also had a problem. It was difficult to get anyone to take her seriously. She was dismissed as an over-anxious, over-protective mother; but finally her doctor did refer her to a famous London hospital, more she felt to set her mind at rest than because he saw anything wrong with the baby.

At the end of a period of in-patient observation her fears were confirmed, and she learned that this second child was also handicapped. She was alone when she was confronted by the specialist team and given the news – someone did ask her if she was all right; but without any further questioning they accepted her assurance that she was. On her way home she was so stunned and overcome with sorrow and despair that she came very near to committing suicide. She never knew what it was that stopped her, but she remembers finding herself thinking, 'So, you've got two handicapped children, children who will never be right . . . but they can't help it, and they are yours. . . . Accept them, love them, enjoy them as much as you can and give them all you can.' She went on to tell us how difficult things had frequently been, how alone she often felt, but also how she had always managed to hold on.

In many ways this mother is the bravest person I have ever had the privilege of knowing. She was undefeated in every way. However, her continuing struggle was immense and would go on until the end of her life. It seemed to be very important to find out if she and all the other parents like her were, in fact, getting all the help they needed, what was being done and what more could be done. Was there no way she could be given enough relief and support to enable her and her husband to enjoy some of the normal pleasures we mostly take for granted? Times have changed, but have they changed enough? If not, what remains to be done and how should we, society in general, set about doing it?

The story of this mother indicates some of the problems faced by the parents of handicapped children and also some of the responses they evoke. With very little support she had already had to come to terms with the fact that her first child would never be normal, and with her own feelings of guilt, anxiety and self-doubt which this knowledge had brought. It was partly the difficulty of dealing with this and the disappointment both she and her husband felt that imposed a great strain on their marriage. She expressed the longing she had felt to have been able to talk to someone who understood. She was able to discuss her anxiety about her younger child with her doctor, and he was sufficiently sympathetic to send her for specialist opinion, but he didn't give her the impression of believing her, so she could talk to him only to a limited extent. Her account of the way she was given the verdict by the hospital raises many questions. Most importantly perhaps it indicates that no one was sufficiently aware of the impact that the news would have on her to do more than ask her if she was all right. One cannot help but wonder how she was told the news and why it was that in a sophisticated hospital she was not given more care and help to assimilate it.

The very fact of parenthood radically alters the parents as people and changes their way of life. If the child is normal it is relatively easy to make the necessary adjustments and to enjoy the enlargement and enrichment of life that a child brings. Life becomes full of new experiences both pleasurable and, at times, painful; there is an extra purpose in life and a different future to look forward to. Included in this is the knowledge that the child will grow up and become in due course an independent being. But if the child is not normal, the picture is very different. From the moment the fact of handicap becomes known or suspected the parents have a complexity of problems to deal with. Perhaps foremost among them is the need to accept this fact and to deal with their own reactions to it, plus the reactions of their partner, their families, neighbours and society in general. A sense of bereavement is always present, although not always consciously recognised. There is mourning for the loss of the child they had hoped to have, closely linked to the demands of the child they have got. In addition to all the emotional problems there are many practical ones. Perhaps above all there is unending anxiety about the future, although this is frequently suppressed because of the pressing demands of day-to-day living.

What help is available? Does the current belief that handicapped children and adults should be kept in the community increase the difficulties? While very few people would still believe that the old institutions are acceptable, how much should community care be held to imply parental or family care? Is too much being demanded of people who through no fault of their own have a handicapped member in the family?

To quote from a letter written by the mother of one: 'The people who make such a fuss about the handicapped's right to life do not realise the burdens parents have to bear. Since Linda's birth I have never been free from anxiety. She is, and always will be, a handicap. She loves me and I love her, but I still wish she had never been born.'

Another mother writes: 'With the best will in the world nobody can truly understand what it is like to have a handicapped child unless you have one yourself. I know I didn't or take any notice of other people's problems until he was born. Then, what an eye-opener.'

In this book the attempt will be made to examine these problems and to consider what is being done to alleviate them, or to make them more tolerable. The problems begin at the time that the fact of handicap is known or suspected. In a book of this length there will not be room to give the problems the full consideration that they deserve, nor to cover all the possible ways of helping them. There are many more than are discussed here. But the book will have served its purpose if it brings some understanding and awareness and helps to lead to the day when no parent will have to say, as did one when discussing this book with me, 'After he was born, my husband and I never went out together anywhere. My own personal freedom was totally inhibited.' Or to ask, as did another, 'If we are willing to care at home most of the time, why is there no help available when we need a break? "Baby-sitting" from a competent person at all stages would have been the biggest help, as we could have had time for a little life of our own.'

'A little life of our own': surely this is not too much to ask for? This book will consider some of the ways it can be achieved.

Finally it should be made clear that, in the main, this book is concerned with the problems of the parents of the more seriously handicapped children. It must not be assumed from this that it is felt that the parents of the less seriously affected have no problems, since this is far from being the case. In fact, many of these parents may well feel that they are facing some of the problems discussed here, although perhaps not always to the same degree of intensity. It would need a far longer book to deal adequately with the whole spectrum, and therefore this one is concentrated on the problems of the parents of the children who will have 'special needs' throughout their lives.

CHAPTER 1

# Birth and Early Years

## Parents Talking

Doctors, particularly clinic doctors, should receive proper training, not only on how to recognise an abnormal child but also how to get this over to parents who are naturally unreceptive to the idea.

The task of dealing with parents in such situations should be given to *experienced* professionals and *not* recently trained ones. Perhaps it would be valuable to evaluate the relationships between professionals and 'clients' in emotional rather than purely clinical terms.

We didn't find out what went wrong at the birth. No one ever sat down to talk to us about it.

When our daughter was born I felt as if I was in a world of my own, not knowing which way to turn. I feel that we should have had more help in coping with our feelings. It would have been nice to have had someone outside the family to talk to. I feel this would have been a great help to us both.

Perhaps the greatest void created was the need for us as parents to adjust our life in emotional terms. Fortunately we were able to cope and obviously were seen as able to cope, but nobody asked us. For fear of interfering?

## Learning the News

Many writers have shown that the majority of expectant parents have transient anxieties, during the period of pregnancy, that the baby may not be normal in some way. Fortunately most of these anxieties prove to be groundless, and the doctor or midwife simply has to answer the other common question, 'Is it a boy or a girl?' But for the minority this is not the case, and someone has to break the news to the parents that their baby has, or may have, some form of handicap or special need. This is clearly not an easy or an enviable task, but it is surely one that should be handled with the utmost skill and delicacy. In fact, this is far from being the case.

One hundred sets of parents recently filled in a questionnaire (a survey undertaken to obtain information for this book), one question of which asked who told them of their child's problem and how it was done. These parents came from different parts of the country and the ages of the children in question ranged from infancy to thirty-plus. The children were representative of four main groups of handicap:

- Rubella-damaged, and deaf/blind children.
- Children with cerebral palsy or associated problems.
- Children with severe learning difficulties.
- Children with behavioural or emotional problems.

The replies, therefore, could not be explained by bad practice in one area or the personalities of the professionals concerned. Eighty-two sets of parents answered this question. Sixty-four of them were told by a doctor or specialist, either at the time of birth or, since handicap is not always apparent immediately, within the first three years. Of the others, two were told by the school doctor when the child first started school, one learned the news when the child was three and admitted to hospital for a tonsillectomy, and one was told by an ophthalmologist when the child was being investigated for suspected bilateral cataracts.

Seventeen sets of parents claimed that they were not told, although they themselves suspected problems and requested that investigations should be made, such investigations subsequently confirming their suspicions. Sometimes this did not happen until the child had started and failed in the ordinary school. Not unnaturally this led to feelings of bitter anger in many of the parents and also to the belief that if they had been listened to sooner their child might have been improved or given the help needed at a much younger age.

As the parents of one boy put it:

> It was not officially recognised that he was handicapped until he was five years old, but we knew that something was wrong when he stopped breathing during a fit at the age of twenty-two months. His speech, which had been quite advanced prior to the fit, suddenly regressed. . . . All we wanted was for the experts to recognise that he had problems and for him to start receiving the necessary help. We were not offered any help and were obviously labelled as over-anxious parents.

Returning to the main group, it therefore appears that, in the main, doctors do accept that the responsibility for telling the parents is theirs. It is difficult to see how it could be otherwise, since they alone have the necessary skill and training to identify abnormalities or causes for suspicion. It is also perfectly correct that they should not make statements based only on suspicions. What is more questionable is their skill in conveying the information or their anxieties. Only one mother of the whole sample expressed complete satisfaction in this respect. She said:

> I was told by the doctor on her ward round. She explained everything thoroughly and made sure that I understood everything she had said and made sure that I was all right. The whole conversation took about thirty-five to forty-five minutes, maybe longer, I can't remember. Approximately ten days later she explained everything again to myself and my husband one Saturday morning. She was very sympathetic and helpful.

This was excellent practice. In the first place the doctor, although on a busy ward round, not only spent time to explain the facts carefully and sympathetically to the mother, but also made sure that the mother had understood them, and that she was all right. Then, most importantly, she repeated the information to both parents after an interval of some days.

Many parents claim that they are not properly told. In some instances this may well be true, but in others it is probably not. It seems to be the case that frequently the parents are told, but at a time and in a way that means they do not take in the information properly. In consequence they later deny they were given it. The first impact of the news can, in one sense, put the parents in a state of shock; and unless this possibility is considered and dealt with in some way, they will subsequently honestly believe they were not told. The doctor, on the other hand, will say correctly that he did tell them.

Of the parents told by the doctors, fifty-eight pairs felt that they were given no help or proper information. These are some typical comments:

> I was just told bluntly.

> I was just told and put out of the office. We were told very coldly, without feeling . . . with our two-and-a-half-year-old daughter there watching her parents get upset. In fact, this has made me very nervous about seeing doctors regarding him [her child with special needs].

> I was told immediately after the birth by a junior paediatrician very awkwardly and embarrassingly. He could give us no help at all.

Only six of these fifty-eight couples were offered even limited help. Three felt that they were given 'vague information', and six felt that the doctors showed 'some sympathy'. The interesting fact, though, is that, although the parents appreciated sympathy when it was tactfully offered, the thing that they nearly all felt most deprived of – and in need of – was real information, both about the nature and extent of the child's problems and practical advice about handling and management. Most of all, they wished to know what could be done to help. It seems that too often they were just baldly told the medical facts or diagnosis.

Some even felt that they had to plead for information and a full diagnosis. Others learned the facts almost in passing or in crueller ways. One father of a Down's syndrome child reported, for example:

> My wife, although faintly suspicious that something was not quite right, had no idea that our child was mentally handicapped until she went to the sister's office a day after the baby was born to borrow the hair-dryer, and there was my daughter's file lying on top of the desk with the words 'mongol tendencies' written clearly in red. . . . Hardly the best way to learn the news.

He went on:

> When I arrived later that day I was met by a grim-faced nurse with the news that my wife was very upset 'and has some very sad news to tell you', but she wouldn't tell me what it was. I immediately thought our daughter had died. A paediatrician then came in to talk briefly to us, but to be honest we were too stunned to take in anything that he said. Apart from that one approach – the only official contact in the hospital – we were given absolutely no other advice or information on how to cope with a handicapped child. It seemed as if the hospital authorities were vaguely embarrassed that it shouldn't have been a normal birth and would be glad to get us off the premises as soon as possible.

This child is now nine, so it might be hoped that things have improved in the interim, but lack of tact and sensitivity is still reported.

The parents of a child now aged two were 'told right away by a paediatrician who was very tactless and said something was wrong with our daughter but now wasn't the time to say more. Some of the nurses were hostile, but others gave more help and sympathy.'

Another mother who was given the news of her daughter's handicap by a paediatrician when the child was six months old said, 'I would like to have been told in a more gentle way than a doctor saying, "Your daughter is spastic." '

There does seem to be evidence that very little appreciation of the parents' feelings is shown. One doctor told the parents bluntly that their day-old baby was handicapped and then added, 'There's always a next time.' There are many other examples which could be quoted, and since some of the children are still very young it cannot be assumed that these examples of bad practice all belong to the past. The following two examples emphasise this point. One mother wrote that, when her baby was six months old, 'I was asked to take my baby to the child clinic at the local hospital, where a paediatrician discussed the child with pupil midwives, and I sat and listened with horror.' This was the first time she had heard the news, and from her report she was not given any sympathy, help or advice following the conference. Another mother was asked to take her child to a case conference at an assessment centre when the baby was seven months old. She was then told of her child's handicap by the paediatrician in the presence of all the conference members. Her GP, who was present, 'avoided us', but other members of the staff were positive and kind afterwards. In the first of these cases the child concerned is now twenty-nine, in the second just six years old.

Three more cases: 'When my son was two he was diagnosed at a London hospital. I [the father] saw the doctor. He just told me that my son was an imbecile, then closed the interview by ringing for the next patient.' The term 'imbecile' shows that this happened some years ago, but the parents of a child now fifteen were simply told by a paediatrician to 'put him away and forget you ever had him', while the parents of a child now aged seven were told when he was ten months old, by a specialist at a major hospital, that the child 'would always be no more than a vegetable'.

Fortunately these later cases are the exception rather than the rule, although this does not mean that they were any less painful to the parents who experienced them. It would be quite unfair to criticise or castigate the majority of the doctors concerned because of them. Yet it does seem fair to say that the majority of doctors are not skilled in communicating the news of handicap to the parents of the affected children. The questions have to be asked: why is this so and what can be done to effect improvement? What do the parents want or feel in need of? There are several possible answers to the first of these questions, but possibly the three main factors can be described briefly as, *personality*, *training* and *experience*.

Dr Mervyn Fox, the author of a pamphlet published by Action Research for the Crippled Child, called *They get this training but they don't really know how you feel* writes:

> The essential craft of medicine is in the diagnosis and treatment of disorder. . . . In so far as human interaction is taught to the apprentice doctor the skill that is considered basic to the proper performance of the craft is that required to take and elicit a clinical history . . . a verbal process designed . . . to enable the doctor to proceed after a physical examination to a clinical diagnosis.[1]

Dr Fox goes on to argue that the art of talking to patients outside the 'context of diagnosis' has to be taught to doctors. Lack of time frequently prevents this, particularly for those doctors who work mainly in the National Health Service, 'where time is at a premium and such conversation may in fact often be regarded as inefficient, because non-productive'. He further points out, while stressing that medical diagnosis and treatment are paramount skills, that nevertheless the role of the doctor *vis-à-vis* the patient is changing. For the patient frequently now requires information and wishes to play a part in decision-making and to have the opportunity of choosing how 'professional skills are utilised on his behalf'. However, many doctors, because of their prolonged and intense habituation in a rigid professional role, cannot regard the patient in this light. The doctor has become a 'prisoner of his training'.

The experiences reported by the majority of the parents in the survey would appear to support this explanation. The fortunate few had as their doctors those who could escape from the 'prison' of their training because either innately or in consequence of their experiences they had emotional sensitivity which made them aware of the total needs of their patients. Most were not so fortunate, however. They were the ones whose doctors carried out their strict professional role; where possible they carried out a diagnosis and then simply communicated it to the parent or parents with no apparent recognition of the effect that the information would have. It is not surprising that nearly every parent expressed the wish to have been told in a different way.

It would seem, therefore, that without being unduly critical of the doctors there is a need for improvements to be made in the way parents are told the news that their child has or may have a problem. A possible first step to effecting this improvement might be to help the doctors to be aware that this need exists. This awareness would have to include some better understanding of the effect that the news is likely to have on the parents. In one sense it is surprising that this sensitivity to the reactions of a patient to information is not a fundamental part of a doctor's training, since by the very nature of their work they are involved as no other professional is in the fundamental matters of life and death, pain and suffering and relief. This does not imply that doctors should be expected to participate in the emotional reactions and responses of their patients; but a conscious awareness of what these feelings are likely to be would surely alter the way in which news is given. This may have an important effect on all that follows. Many doctors do appreciate these facts, and some courses are now being set up to help them to improve their communication skills. Unfortunately they are still too few and far between.

## Reactions to the News

Handicapped children are born to parents in every stratum of society. Therefore there is not one group which can be treated as an entity. Each parent will react in their own individual way and should be offered the understanding and help appropriate to them alone. Nevertheless it does seem to be possible to recognise a pattern of responses which, subject to the above proviso, is commonly experienced. This seems to fall into four different stages:

1. *The immediate reaction* is usually one of shock and anger coupled with disbelief. The following comments are typical of those made at this stage:

> We felt shattered, disappointed, angry, sorry, bewildered, outraged and confused. We felt disgusted with life and felt that life was not worth living.

> I felt very bitter and depressed.

> I felt shocked and a numbness that lasted for about twenty-four hours. I felt that life was unfair.

> We felt shocked. At first we did not believe it was true.

> We were completely shattered, devastated, heart-broken and terribly hurt. We suffered together – what faith I had went. My feelings went so deep I couldn't describe them.

2. After the initial period of shock, *a period of mourning* takes place and also a period of isolation when the parents feel remote from reality. Frequently they also feel a wish to be left alone. Typical comments:

> My husband was grief-stricken. I was unable to accept the possibility.

> I felt guilty and that I was being punished for making a bad marriage.

> I [the mother] was completely wrapped up in the problem. His father pretended the problem didn't exist. For about eighteen months we drifted apart and dealt with the problem in our own way.

> We couldn't for some time talk to each other about our son, but we tried to protect each other from the hurt.

> I found that I did not want to be with people who did not know about our son. I could not bear the explanations, reactions, sympathy. I wallowed in self-pity in private, and kept a bright social face when I needed to.

3. *A period of adaption* occurring when the parents are emerging from the period of intense grief and begin, sometimes frantically, to try to come to terms with the situation and also to try to find ways in which they can help their child. Typical comments:

> I felt and still feel that it is a challenge.

> I wanted to be told more about my child's handicap and advised how to deal with it. I was kept in the dark during the early years.

> I wanted more professional help and understanding from health visitors, for example, and more practical help on how to motivate my child with special needs. Also help with motivating myself to motivate an unresponsive child.

> I wanted help not to feel alone.

4. *Adjustment*. Some parents do not reach this stage but remain fixed in one of the earlier ones. For those who do, life does become a little easier. Typical comments:

> Once I felt able to meet friends and relatives and told them she was handicapped, we were able to meet the hurdles as a family.

> All children are special and with special needs. We adapted quickly to what our son required, and it is only now that we feel he has made a difference as to how we might otherwise have led our lives. A complete change of life was not easy, but we are learning to cope, and indeed enjoy him as we learn to accept our son's situation.

> The reality of having a handicapped child takes a while to adjust to . . . and it is all such an unknown quantity. By the third birthday it is fairly obvious how

handicapped a child will be – no longer a baby but requiring baby needs. The best thing we did was to have more children to maintain a normal family and to keep life in proportion. When days were difficult I felt that I had to keep up a 'front' to protect myself and my family. But had I wilted, sat and cried, my whole world would have collapsed, so through all difficulties I had to be strong.

These are the main stages of reaction that the parents go through. But underlying everything else and normally for the rest of their lives many seem to feel that from the moment their 'special' child was born they ceased to be part of the normal community, that in some way they were fixed and set apart from the rest of humanity and that the way everyone else regards them has been radically altered. One mother puts it like this: 'What we really needed, and need, is just to be treated and listened to as normal persons, not as handicapped people.'

From this and other similar evidence it seems that there is a definite need for everyone to re-examine their attitudes towards handicap, and that this applies to the professionals who are dealing with the families as much as it does to the community at large. There are a minority of parents who need special consideration, and these fall into two categories. Firstly, there are those who honestly and sincerely decide that they cannot take the handicapped child home to become part of the family. It is a simple fact that not everybody or every family can cope with a handicapped member. Secondly, there are those who have to make an almost immediate decision whether or not to consent to an operation which may save or prolong the child's life. Sometimes this decision has to be made even during pregnancy. A mother known to be carrying a handicapped baby, for instance, is offered the possibility of abortion.

Another example was recently provided in a poignant letter published in one of the daily newspapers. It was written purely to console other parents who felt guilty because they found themselves wishing that their severely handicapped child had never been born, and it described this dilemma in a way that no one could unless they had experienced it personally. The letter described how, in the eighth month of pregnancy, the parents were told that their child would be born severely subnormal. The doctors gave them the choice of either having a caesarean birth immediately – in which case the child would be born alive – or letting the pregnancy continue, with the certainty that the baby would die at birth. Fortunately, for this is not always the case, the parents were able to come to a joint decision which they found the hardest and yet the easiest they had ever had to make. They decided to let the pregnancy take its course, and, as the doctors had foretold, the baby died during the birth. Emotionally the parents were devastated, but they were sustained in their grief by the knowledge that they had made their decision purely out of love and concern for their baby. The point they were making was that they felt no parent should feel guilt if they wished their child dead, rather than having to endure a life of 'torment, trial and sadness'.

The period immediately after the birth of a severely handicapped child is the time when the parents are in the maximum state of confusion, grief, guilt and despair and are also very vulnerable. However, it is sometimes then that they have to decide whether or not to consent to an operation which may save or prolong the life of the child – a child who will always need constant care and attention. Both these parents and those who decide that they cannot live with a handicapped child are in a dilemma which has no right or wrong answer. As the persons most affected, however (apart from the child, who is quite unable to contribute), they must make the decision. It sometimes happens that others, people of strong convictions, intervene, with what they consider to be the best of motives. Then if the operation is carried out and is successful, the parents have to make another heart-breaking decision as to the child's future.

This whole issue is one that people do feel strongly about. It could be endlessly debated and never resolved. One thing does seem clear, however, and that is that moral judgements should never be expressed to add to the parents' load. They should be offered nothing but information, sympathy and understanding and never be met with implicit or explicit disapproval.

## Notes

1. A. Mervyn Fox, *They get this training but they don't really know how you feel*, Horsham, Action Research for the Crippled Child, 1974, Introduction, pp. 1–2.

CHAPTER 2

# Dealing with the News

## Parents Talking

As with all the other parents of handicapped children, we have had an enormous amount of struggles, unpleasant experiences, pleasant experiences, laughter and tears.

In hindsight I now feel strongly that if I had been helped to understand my son's handicap in his first formative years much unnecessary pain would have been avoided.

We wanted constructive help, support and advice as to how we could help our son.

We wanted more professional understanding and sympathy from our health visitor and more practical help in how to deal with the child.

I do believe parents respond well to practical suggestions as to how to help the child. Their frustrations are greatly lessened if they feel they are doing something positive.

We would have liked contact with other parents with like problems. This contact comes *much later*, and yet it is of prime importance.

I suspected brain damage soon after birth, but this was not confirmed until my child was two years old. Everyone said I was very lucky to have such a placid baby.

We felt sadness and an extra special love for the baby, and pity.

## Dealing with the News

One of the most devastating events that can happen in a family is the birth of a

> handicapped child. How the parents accept and adjust to the situation will largely depend upon *how* they are told, *when* they are told and the measure of support they receive in the early days following diagnosis.
>
> (Barbara Crowe, parent-counsellor/liaison social worker)[1]

Chapter 1 showed that there is room for much improvement in the way parents are told. What of the measure of support? Today there are many agencies which do operate to offer help, advice and support to the parents of handicapped children, but on the whole they do not operate immediately after the child is born. It is almost as if at the time of greatest need little is available.

In the questionnaire previously referred to the parents were asked whether they were offered any help in dealing with the news of the baby's handicaps and also what help or assistance they would like to have had offered to them. Very few – less than 10 per cent – felt that they had received any help; and those who said they had in the main got it from their immediate family or close friends. Over and over again it was stated that the things they wanted most of all were (1) fuller information, (2) someone to talk to and (3) practical advice as to what they could do to improve their child's condition and future prospects.

The following are typical comments:

> I wanted someone to talk to familiar with our problem, and to have some idea of the future.

> We wanted someone to talk to in the first few months about the problems we were going to have with her.

> We wanted to talk but were not given the chance. I feel that we should have had more help with our feelings. It would have been nice to have had someone outside the family to talk to. I feel that this would have been a great help to my husband and myself.

All of the parents felt that they were suddenly faced with the unknown. They had to come to terms with their own feelings, and almost invariably this involved a lack of confidence in their ability to look after their child and to be good parents. Much of their loss of self-confidence was due to their feeling of not knowing what to expect. At the same time many were also dealing with their wish to reject the baby. It has been suggested that some degree of rejection is always present and that this can range from a total rejection of the *child* (for example: 'Initially my baby was a beautifully looked-after baby whom I loathed') to a wish to reject because of the parents' own feeling of inadequacy ('We wanted more help from properly qualified people with whom we could discuss things, but we were not given the chance to do so. We needed advice, information and counselling').

Fortunately there is a growing awareness of this need and of the fact that parents need help as soon as possible after being given the diagnosis. For example, a local action group from East Surrey, which consists of professionals and representatives of voluntary societies working with the mentally handicapped, states:

> The Action Group believes that improved support and counselling during the first year or so could have an important influence on parental attitudes towards caring for and promoting the development of their children. The local MENCAP societies have expressed concern that once parents are told of their child's handicap not enough is done to make sure that they have access to all the information and services available.[2]

Although perhaps more could be done by some of the paediatricians who first give the news, it would be unrealistic to expect that they would have either the time or opportunity to continue to deal with all the parents. Someone else should be available to offer the help that is needed, and this help should be available as a matter of course, rather than it being a matter of chance depending upon which professionals are dealing with the parents or where they happen to live. Three main ways are developing in which this help is offered and is available. Firstly, there are the parent groups, secondly the community centres and thirdly family centres.

**Parent Groups**

From the evidence available it seems that many of the parents felt that the person they could most easily talk to would be someone who had shared the same experience – that is, a parent of a child with similar handicaps. Margaret Brock, in her moving book, *Christopher: A Silent Life*, puts it this way: 'in the early days of devastation only someone who has themselves been through a similar experience can be of help. The time for expert help comes a little later.'[3] Barbara Crowe, in her unpublished discussion paper, makes the same point when she says:

> If parents are going to accept a handicapped baby and all the ensuing responsibilities, they need to be assured that they are not alone and that help is available. Whatever professional help is available, most parents gain considerable benefit from an opportunity to talk to a parent of a child with a similar handicap.[4]

The effect such help has on the new parents is described vividly by one mother who received it. She had been full of dread and unanswered questions when her Down's syndrome baby was born. 'I kept thinking that I would wake up at any moment and find it was all a terrible dream. The nightmare was for real, it was happening, and I didn't know what to do or where to turn.' Fortunately she lived in a neighbourhood where 'within thirty-six hours of our daughter's birth help was at hand'. After they had been visited by the local Medical Officer of Health and the mother who worked with him as a parent-counsellor she says of herself and her husband, 'We felt so very different then. There was so much that could be done.' As they had promised, the visitors 'came back again and answered all our questions. More important, they sat and listened to us talking, and *understood*.'

Parent groups have, therefore, developed from a deep-felt need. Where they exist, their value is inestimable. An excellent example of such a group and the way in which one can be set up is to be found in the one run by the Southend Society for the Mentally Handicapped.

**The Southend Group**

This group was started in 1970 under the leadership of Dr Mellor, the then Deputy Medical Officer of Health, who had working with him as observers a psychiatric social worker and the head of what was then a junior training centre. The first group consisted of six couples, all with a child with severe learning difficulties, and ran for sixteen successive weeks. At the end of that time it was decided that the work should continue, and further groups were set up. Developments took place, one of the most important being that it was found desirable to set up specific groups to meet specific needs. The experience of the first group had shown that parents had differing needs at different stages of their child's development. As the number of groups grew, there were not enough professionals with the time available to lead each group, so a system was set up to train and select parents as group leaders.

These leaders are chosen partly for their depth of experience, in that they are the parents of an older child with a similar handicap to that of the children of the parents in each particular group, and partly for their qualities of leadership. They are always participating members of the group and, in fact, almost select themselves as leaders from the manner of their participation. The training takes place within the group situation, coming partly from the leader of the group first attended and partly from the visiting professionals who attend the groups to join in the discussions and to explain their particular work. These professionals include paediatricians, a consultant in subnormality, teachers, speech therapists, educational psychologists, social workers and health visitors. There is overall guidance from the medical adviser, who is also president of the Southend Society for the Mentally Handicapped. The leaders are trained to attend to such points as ensuring that a parent can talk without interruption and that all join in the general discussion, with no 'pairing' taking place. It is also considered important to ensure that parents do answer any questions put to them, rather than allow them to evade an issue. Typical of the topics discussed are day-to-day problems, e.g. of feeding, problems with siblings and of family management. Simple techniques of behaviour modification are also dealt with. It has been found useful to have present an observer who does not join in the discussions but notes anything relevant (for example, if something seems to be going wrong) and then discusses them with the leader after the session has ended. Great importance is put on the fact that the group leaders must be willing and able to act in complete co-operation with the professionals and any other agencies that might become involved. They must in every sense be regarded as, and regard themselves as, part of a team who will become part of the life of the family.

The groups meet regularly and, as discussed above, are visited at intervals by professional people who contribute to the discussions from their own expertise and experience. But, as Barbara Crowe says, 'The greatest help is gained from meeting each other regularly to share problems and successes. Whatever the problem, there is always someone else in the group who has had a similar problem and so can be of help.'

A special feature of the Southend Group, and one which seems to be very necessary in the eyes of the parents, is that it is organised to provide a visit to parents within forty-eight hours of the birth or diagnosis of handicap. The babies concerned at present are all Down's syndrome, since this is a condition which can be diagnosed with certainty at an early age. The new parents are asked if they would like a visit from the parent of a child with the same handicap as their own. Almost invariably the answer is 'yes' and when it is given it is promptly followed by the proposed visit. It should be stressed again that the visiting parent is working with the doctors involved and has had training in acting as a parent-counsellor. If the parents wish, a second visit takes place within forty-eight hours, and then the parents are told about the groups and invited to join the next meeting of the 0–2 group. It is only at a later stage that they are told about the local Society, and no pressure is put upon them at any time to join. The option is open to them if and when they wish to follow it up.

Southend now has a newly formed District Community Mental Health Team. Full discussions with this team take place to ensure that there is complete co-operation between the two agencies. This helps to prevent the parents being 'swamped' with too many agencies which may with the best of intentions be giving conflicting advice. This, of course, would lead only to confusion for the parents before they had even begun to come to terms with their new situation.

The Group and the Community Team have agreed the following system for early counselling:

1. The consultant paediatrician is alerted immediately such a baby is born. As soon as possible both parents are told together of the diagnosis. It is felt to be very important that, unless the father is no longer involved with the mother, he should be present when the news is given.
2. Referral from maternity unit to the GP, health visitor and District Mental Health Team.

3. At the time the diagnosis is given, a visit from the parent-counsellor is offered straight away, and then the parent-counsellor is called in if the parents agree.

Since the work of the Southend Group became known, a number of similar combinations of early visiting and parent groups for children of 0 to 2 years have been set up elsewhere, as for instance in Basildon, Havering, Chelmsford, Edinburgh and Nottingham. They are not identical with the Southend Group, nor would this be advisable, because each group has to be appropriate to the local conditions. An essential factor whenever a society wishes to set up such a group is that close co-operation must first be established with the local authority and hospitals; for it is believed that in no other way could the statutory bodies feel confident to use the voluntary workers.

When a scheme such as the one described above is operating, the parents, who choose to use it derive great support and comfort from it, but such schemes are far from being universally available. They are very dependent on there being in the neighbourhood parents who are able to conceive of such a scheme and, in spite of their own needs and responsibilities, have the energy to initiate it. The other crucial factor is, of course, that the local medical and other professionals must accept and value the help that such parents' groups can offer. It is not always the case that these things operate; however, there are a growing number of acceptable alternatives. Of these, the scheme that seems to offer the best possibility of making help available to all the parents who need it is the growing number of Community Health Teams. These teams, where they exist, were formed to facilitate the coordination of the various services involved into a unified service, with common practices existing for all disciplines in caring for mentally handicapped persons within one area. If and when this service has been established in every area, it should be a way in which the parents of all handicapped children are offered support and advice.

## Community Health Services

When a baby is born who can immediately be identified as being handicapped (which, of course, is not always the case) the paediatrician concerned sends notification of the birth to the Senior Medical Officer of Health in the area. If the handicap is a physical one then the child is referred to the specialist dealing with that particular handicap, who then assumes care and determines subsequent events. If the handicap is a mental one then the referral is to the local Community Mental Handicap Team.

A typical example of this kind of team and its operational policy is that set up by East Surrey – see Figure 1. This is a comprehensive service intended to provide for the people it serves from birth to the end of their lives. Its two specific aims are stated as follows:

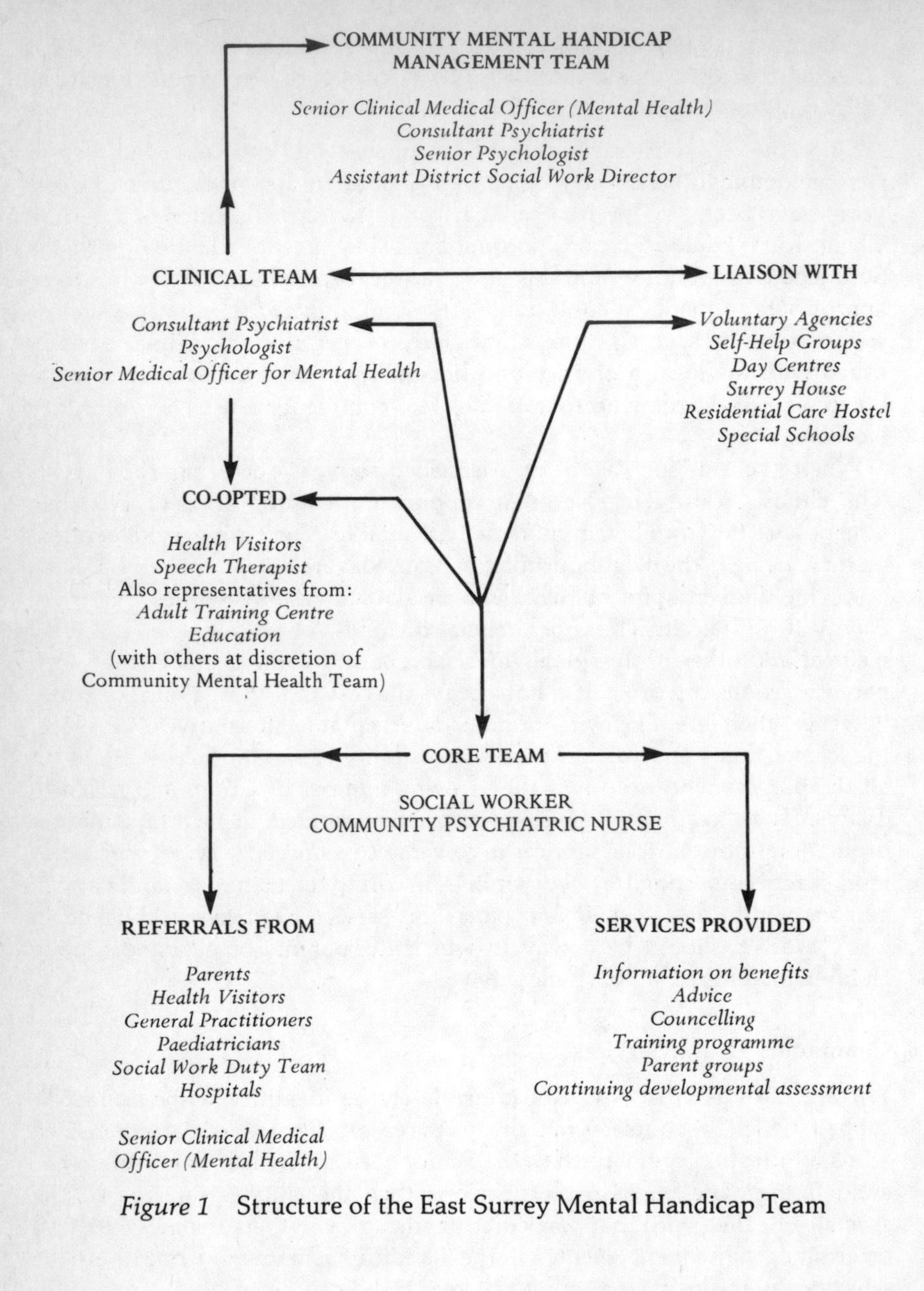


*Figure 1* Structure of the East Surrey Mental Handicap Team

1. To provide supportive services to mental handicap clients and their families and to co-ordinate these services.
2. To improve the quality of their lives and maximise their potential.

Allied to these it has a list of six objectives, all of which have been designed to further the two main aims.[5] The team is structured and divided into (a) the Core Team, who are in direct contact with the families, (b) the Clinical Team, of which the Core Team forms a part, and (c) the Management Team.

*The Core Team*

There are three Core Teams in the district in question, each working in one area. Each team consists of a minimum of a social worker and a community nurse working with the co-operation and support of other relevant services, which can include health visitors, speech therapists, physiotherapists and so on. The use of the other services is in theory determined by the needs of the child/client and his or her family. Unfortunately at the present time a very relevant factor is the availability of the professionals or services needed; and, as the people concerned are only too aware, 'demand' usually exceeds 'supply'. The role of the Core Team is to deal with referrals, to know and to visit the families and to decide which cases need to be assessed or reassessed by the Clinical Team. It is from this group that a key worker is chosen for every family. She or he will be the one directly involved with the family and, hopefully, the one to whom the family feels able to talk and to turn to for advice. The key worker can be any member of the team and wherever possible the person chosen is the one felt to be most likely to be accepted by a particular family.

The members of this team are also responsible for arranging emergency facilities and keeping up the Mental Handicap Register. They meet as a group fortnightly and as a team are directly responsible to the Clinical Team. Their role does not replace that of the health visitor, who will continue to visit the family in the normal way and may, in fact, be co-opted as a member of the Core Team, even at times assuming the role of key worker. The important thing is that communication is established between the different services and co-operation ensured as far as possible. Basically, however, the health visitor as a key member of the primary health team has a specific role to play. Her or his involvement with a family may well start during pregnancy for if this can be arranged she or he will be able to establish at this stage her or his supportive role and also, if it is wanted, give advice on preparation for parenthood and so on. If for one reason or another this is not the case, the involvement will begin when the baby is about ten days old, when the first home visit is made. During this visit the health visitor is not only getting to know the family but also assessing their circumstances and needs, while at the same time offering her or his services at any time the need is felt for advice. Until the child is five, routine visits will be made to the home, and the family will also be seen at the child health clinics. The health visitor works in partnership with the GP, and it is part of her or his task to give advice on health matters and to carry out child development assessments.

Although they are not concerned only with the young, most health visitors consider that primary preventive care of young families should come high on their list of priorities. Their task is essentially to identify needs and then refer them to the appropriate agencies. Their task would become impossible if they were expected to fulfil all these needs, even if they had the necessary expertise and access to the facilities. They are in the unique position of being the professional who initiates contacts with families rather than having to depend upon referrals; normally they are the ones in the position to make the referrals. The health visitor is therefore an important link upon whom depends communication and to some extent co-operation between the agencies and with the families. There is no reason why they should act only in this capacity, however, if it is desirable for them to play a fuller role and they wish to do so. The main obstacle may well be that they do not have the time available.[6]

*The Clinical Team*

The Clinical Team consists of the Core Team plus the consultant psychiatrist, the psychologist, the Senior Medical Officer for Mental Health and various co-opted members as required. These may include medical social workers, health visitors, speech therapist, physiotherapist and, where appropriate, representatives from a special school or social training centre or workshop. This team is accountable to the Community Mental Handicap Team. It has two main activities:

1. *To run an outpatient clinic* weekly or fortnightly where in an informal setting the parents can go with their handicapped child for additional help, support, advice or counselling. The key worker has the responsibility of instigating the visit and also of getting whatever information the Clinical Team may require.
2. *To meet monthly*. At these meetings the appointment of all key workers is discussed and confirmed. The main purpose of the meeting is, however, to discuss and agree upon the treatment plans and the management and care of the families in their area. It is a meeting of specialist professionals combining their expertise to ensure that each family can get the most appropriate form of help.

Presiding over the whole service is the Management Team.

*Community Mental Handicap Management Team*

This team consists of the Senior Clinical Medical Officer (Mental Health), the consultant psychiatrist, the assistant district social work director and the senior psychologist. The team meets quarterly and has three main tasks:

1. To review and update procedures for the Core Teams and the Clinical Teams.
2. To identify any shortfalls or imbalances in service provision in the area, and to evaluate the service being provided in comparison with the national norm.
3. To pass on the information it has to the Mental Handicap Service Team for planning and development. All aspects of the work done have been planned in detail to ensure that nothing has been overlooked.

An example of this is the way in which referrals can be made and followed up. They are usually made on a prescribed card or by letter to any member of the Core Team and can come from a wide variety of sources, e.g. hospitals, special schools, relatives or any other person associated with the care of the mentally handicapped. To ensure that all are recorded, they are checked with the Mental Handicap Register. Home visits are made, and family clinics held, with the relevant GP always being informed if one of his or her patients is being seen. Conferences which have relevance to the care offered are attended. Short-term relief can be provided. Importantly there is a twenty-four-hour cover service available to any parent or client who is unable to contact their key worker in time of need.

The type of service and care described above is systematised and planned in such a way that for those it serves, i.e. the mentally handicapped, it should do much to provide the care and assistance the parents feel in such need of. But it is new in its present form and is being designed and set up at a time of great economic stringency. It is extremely unlikely that sufficient funds will be available to ensure that enough resources, both practical and personal, will be provided to meet the whole needs of the service. To some extent it will remain the model to be worked towards. The Southend experience shows how it can be complemented by an active parents' group. Both of these services largely deal with the needs of the mentally handicapped. This is by far the largest group of handicap, so it is nearly always possible in all but the smallest and most remote communities to organise a local parents' group when a sufficient number feel the need for one. This is not the case with all the handicaps; as one mother sadly said, 'It does seem to be the case that the more complex and severe your child's problems are, the less they are catered for.'

As has been discussed already in this chapter, the parents of a child who is mentally handicapped do have some prospect of getting help, support and contact with other parents. This is not necessarily the case for the parents of children with other forms of handicap. It is simplistic to believe that children who are affected necessarily fall into one of two clear-cut categories, mentally handicapped or physically handicapped. Also, it can take years for a complete picture of a child's problems to be formed.

A child with a suspected or obvious physical problem becomes the patient of the relevant specialist, who from then on is a key figure in the life of that child and his or her family. This is perhaps especially true in the first months or even years when diagnosis is taking place. Parents are therefore almost in a no man's land as far as getting assistance is concerned until a possible diagnosis has been reached. They are also in a state of continuing anxiety, either knowing or suspecting that there is something wrong but having no real information. It is not unknown either for a GP, if turned to for advice, to be dismissive of a parent's fears.

The mother of a child who proved eventually to have a severe handicap commented:

> Basically I needed help in convincing professionals that I had a 'special child'. I was fobbed off with being a first-time neurotic mother. When my GP's wife (also a doctor) told me at my son's three-month check-up that I hadn't bonded with my baby and hence his screaming, I flipped. I had anti-depressants and valium for about two months.

She was not alone in being offered anti-depressants when all she wanted was for her fears to be taken seriously, investigated and discussed. Other parents report similar experiences. The worried parents of an adopted child were not told until he was two years old that he had cerebral palsy, although they constantly sought help. Even after they were told, little help was available.

The very fact that diagnosis can, and frequently does, take years to complete is one of the main reasons why doctors cannot always respond to an anxious parent's questions and at times appear to be evading, belittling or ignoring them. Until diagnosis is complete, the doctor or specialist has to decide how much it is correct to disclose. It is a difficult balance that has to be struck, but no doctor would feel justified in making a statement about a child's condition until he or she felt that there was the necessary evidence. The trouble is that the uncertainty of the situation can lead to destructive anxiety for the parents. A compromise has in many cases appeared to be the best answer. False reassurance is useless; but as one parent put it, 'If only we had been treated as normal and told by the doctor that he did not know at that time, we would have been able to cope, especially if he could have explained to us what he was going to do to find out. We did learn all these things in time, but by then it was almost too late.'

The great improvements in diagnostic techniques that are being made will also help to improve the situation, because the long period of waiting to find out can be considerably reduced by them. An interesting example of this is the 'motion cradle' developed to help in the diagnosis of possible hearing loss which can be used at a very early age, since nothing in the way of co-operation is required from the child. Briefly, it works as follows. The infant is placed in a cradle, and his or her spontaneous movements are electrically recorded until a base pattern of normal behaviour is recorded, both while the child is awake and when he or she is asleep. Auditory stimuli are then introduced, and any change of movement brought about by them is automatically recorded. A lack of response or a poor response is evidence that this baby has some degree of hearing loss, while a good response proves that this is not the case.

A modified attitude by the doctors and the advantages gained from improved diagnostic techniques will help with the parents' emotional trauma. But they will not give them the contact with other parents that seems to be so valuable. This is where family centres can fill the gap.

## Family Centres

Family centres can be initiated by the parents but they require a great deal of effort in the early stages, because usually there will not be enough parents living closely together to form a neighbourhood group. A centre to which parents from different areas can travel to meet together can be the answer. These centres usually cater for children with the same or related handicaps. Two typical ones are White Lodge Centre in Chertsey, mainly for children with cerebral palsy, and the Family Centre in Ealing, which is for deaf/blind and rubella-damaged children. Alternatively as at Honeylands in Exeter they can cater for children with a wide range of special needs. Honeylands is also an example of a centre which has been developed within a general practice service. One important feature common to all three of these centres is that, in addition to providing a meeting place for the parents, they all offer professional advice and support.

### *White Lodge Centre*

White Lodge Centre is affiliated to the Spastics Society but is a separate charity which was founded by parents' efforts and drive over thirty years ago. From its humble beginnings in a village hall it has developed into a comprehensive service housed in a purpose-built centre on an attractive site. It is open to all who can get there, but because of transport problems the children who attend come mainly from a large part of Surrey and the adjoining parts of Hampshire. Education is provided for twenty-four children, with a further twenty-four in the nursery. Sixteen other children attend as out-patients for therapy and treatment. Others who have moved on from White Lodge to other schools and units come periodically for medical advice. There is a fully staffed therapy centre where physiotherapy, speech therapy and hydrotherapy are among the services provided. Recently the work has been extended by the opening of an adult centre, which it is planned to develop into a 'centre for living'. All the departments are run by fully qualified staff. Three paediatricians visit White Lodge Centre. The needs of the parents are not forgotten, for support and advice are freely available to them. The aim is to have all the staff working closely together to meet the particular needs of each child, and to encourage the children to develop fully their individual abilities.

What White Lodge means to the parents is expressed by one who, writing in their own journal and calling herself a 'Spastic Mum', put it the following way:

> When my daughter and I joined the White Lodge family . . . it was as though we were carried into a different world and a world of kindness and dedication. . . . My daughter has benefited tremendously from the care, attention and stimulation she has received from the staff. She and I can now converse because we are learning a common language, which means that she is no longer isolated or screeching with frustration, and that is heavenly for all of us.
>
> I am also impressed with the willingness of the White Lodge staff to try to help and cope with the needs and frustrations of families in distress. One of the unfortunate side-effects of a disability like cerebral palsy is that it can handicap a family. It is comforting to know that you are not fighting the battles alone, that there are people (staff and other parents) who can understand your situation and will try to give you whatever support they can. . . . Although I am not happy about her affliction I'm not ashamed of it either. My acceptance of the problem is wholly due to the 'White Lodge Family'.[7]

It would be superfluous to add any comment to this statement, but the sad thing is that White Lodges are not available to all who need them, as is also the case with the next centre to be described.

### *The Family Centre*

The Family Centre was opened in 1980 by the National Association for Deaf/Blind and Rubella Handicapped (NAD/BRH) to provide services for families having a child with a dual sensory handicap. The NAD/BRH was founded in 1955 by a group of parents who felt the need to meet and discuss with other parents whose children had similar handicaps. Once again, as with White Lodge, it is through the drive and energy of these first parents that it has grown into a very active association. It has brought about many improvements in the provisions being made for these multiply handicapped children and also a growing demand for the elimination of the disease causing the handicaps, namely rubella. Since 1970 there has been a safe and effective vaccine, and if all prospective mothers were immunised very few if any children would be damaged by the congenital rubella syndrome. This is an aim and a hope for the future; meanwhile much remains to be done for the children who have been so tragically affected. The Association (now known as SENSE) has for some time been involved in a long-running 'saga' trying to get better educational provision for these children with such very special needs.

The Family Centre is one of the major improvements SENSE has achieved. It is uniquely still the only centre in the country specifically catering for deaf/blind children and their families. The only criterion for admission is that the child should have the dual sensory handicap. An individual developmental programme is drawn up for each child based on his or her own needs and those of the family. Its aim is to stimulate the child to use all his or her abilities and to develop for the child the acquisition of such visual, auditory, tactile, motor-communication and self-help skills as he or she is capable of. Since the children come from many parts of Britain one of the main aims is to help the parents to become effective teachers of their own child. Accommodation is available in the Centre for those who need it, and other members of the family plus any teachers or therapists who wish to accompany the child and his or her parents are welcome. Home visits are made by three peripatetic teachers based at the Centre, and by means of these and the visits to the Centre the programmes are constantly being reviewed and updated.

The Centre also acts as an advisory service which covers all aspects of help from suggestions of suitable toys and stimulating activities to advice and information on statutory services and voluntary provision. Parents are also kept in touch and informed by means of a news-sheet which circulates among the members and always includes parents' accounts of their children. As with the parents of the White Lodge children, these parents also feel no longer alone but members of a caring and supportive 'family'.[8]

Both White Lodge and the Family Centre are the creation of parents who have evolved them to meet their common needs. The parents gain a lot from them but they also contribute a great deal to them, not least is the constant effort that has to be put into fund-raising. There is no doubt of the value of these centres, and it is quite understandable that the parents wish to retain control of them, since they are the fruits of their own experience. It does seem, however, that the time has come to discuss whether they cannot be relieved of some of the financial burden. If they had chosen not to look after their children themselves and society in general had to take up their care, not only would the life of the children be far less happy but the cost would be prohibitive. Would it not be possible to use some of the money thus saved to provide and extend nation-wide the facilities and services that these and similar centres provide?

### *Honeylands*

Honeylands, a family support unit in Exeter, based on the wishes and needs of parents, has been developed as part of a general paediatric service. It was originally founded by one doctor who saw a need and actively set about fulfilling it. It is housed in a separate building on a large hospital site, described in the booklet given to the parents when they are introduced to Honeylands as 'old and in some ways rather grand with a lovely garden and adventure playground'.[9] Perhaps the very first page of this booklet sets the tone, for it says: 'We find that families use Honeylands in many different ways – we aim to be flexible enough to help you. Please let us know how best Honeylands can provide a useful service for your family.' It offers this service and support to families of children with a wide variety of special needs.

Most of the children start to visit before the age of five and are referred by their own doctor because they have some 'difficulty with walking, talking or one of the other skills that small children have to learn'. Some children visit every weekday, others only once a month. The main emphasis is placed on helping the parents to acquire both the confidence and the skills they need to help their children. They are welcome to visit as and when they will, and have at their disposal a room where they meet and talk to each other and exchange ideas and experiences. There is a full specialist advisory staff, all of whom are available to the parents on request. The introductory booklet explains their separate roles. As with the other centres described, the dual aim is to cater for the parents' needs and by so doing to help them help their children to reach their maximum potential.

Honeylands offers a fully comprehensive service; for in addition to all the other facilities, the staff say:

> We hope that we can help simply by looking after individual children occasionally. We hope that as parents get to know us they will be able to trust us with their children for a day or a night, for a weekend or for a fortnight's holiday. . . . We believe that it is important that there are times when parents can leave their child with us so that they can do things as a family that they could not otherwise do.

The relief for the parents of knowing that this is the case is great, for otherwise the lack of this kind of facility is one of the many constant anxieties they have to live with. If proof of the value of such a service were to be needed, the fact that about two hundred families in East Devon make use of it is surely evidence enough. Honeylands also offers an inspiring example of what can be done within the statutory services if the imagination and will are there.

### Conclusions

In this chapter the needs and wishes expressed by the parents on hearing the news of their child's handicap have been considered, and examples have been given of some of the ways they are, and can be, met. These examples have been used because they are succeeding, but the list is not comprehensive. Even so it would be quite wrong to give the impression that the sort of services described can be found everywhere. Ultimately the hope is that this will be the case, but at times progress does seem to be abysmally slow. It is however very important that these precedents have been set and shown to succeed, and that it has also been shown that there are different ways in which parents' needs can be successfully met.

## Notes

1. Barbara Crowe, unpublished discussion paper, Southend Group, 1982.
2. East Surrey Action Group, 'Mental handicap in East Surrey, provisions, problems and priorities for change', unpublished report, 1982, p. 4.
3. Margaret Brock, *Christopher: A Silent Life*, London, Bedford Square Press, 1975 and 1984, p. 65.
4. See above, note 1.
5. East Surrey Community Mental Handicap Teams, unpublished operational policy statement pp. 25–9.
6. Conference report, *The Role of the Health Visitor*, North-East London Polytechnic, 1981; copies available from Special Course Office.
7. White Lodge Family Centre, *Year Book*, 1984, p. 43.
8. Leaflets, etc., about the Ealing Family Centre are obtainable from SENSE (the National Association for Deaf/Blind and Rubella Handicapped), 311 Gray's Inn Road, London WC1X 8PT.
9. Introduction to Honeylands booklet; available from Honeylands, Pinhoe Road, Exeter, Devon.

CHAPTER 3

# Effects on Relationships

**Parents Talking**

We were heart-broken, but in total oneness. The demands on us both made life intense. We expected a great deal more of the other children.

My husband was supportive – we were close to each other, but I found that I resented that he was able to escape by going to work.

We blamed each other and almost split up.

It drew us together – but kept us apart.

My husband and I have probably suffered by my sadness and pessimism. He too is sad but escapes to work. Our whole family life has suffered in more ways than one.

My husband was a great comfort.

I felt guilty and frightened and apart from my husband. We were very hurtful to each other.

Because my child's needs were so demanding I became aggressive to the other children. I couldn't give the other children so much of my time.

Our sexual life was curtailed.

We had less time for our daughter and each other. Our social life and general relations with our friends were adversely affected.

We couldn't do much as a family. We had to plan visits carefully, and often one parent would do something with the older children while the other looked after the handicapped one.

We had a job to do as a family. Sharing this drew us together.

> We were young, and I spent all my time with the baby, as I felt more for him. We drifted apart and then got divorced.

> I never wanted to stop talking about our son and his problems, and my husband never wanted to start. Many years later when we could speak with ease, my husband said how much he used to dread to come home to my 'eternal dirge' about our son and he felt his happy wife was gone for ever.

> When you are the parent of a handicapped child, your whole life, social and professional, and that of your family, changes completely.

> I don't know one parent of a handicapped child who doesn't feel guilty about having one. . . . It is hard to say how it affects you, save to say that it is probably the worst thing that can happen to anyone – the one thing that stays with you always. The pain never diminishes. As the child grows, the handicap becomes more obvious and affects the whole family more. You have to be very tough.

The last two comments, from two mothers, are typical of those made by an overwhelming number of the parents of handicapped children. The birth of any child radically alters a family, effecting changes in relationships, situations and finances. To this extent there is nothing unusual in the situation as regards the parents of a handicapped child, but it would be extremely foolish to pretend there is no difference. It is important to analyse what the differences are – are they differences of kind, or of intensity?

It is often said, and sometimes by the parents, that a handicapped child inevitably creates a handicapped family. Clearly there is much truth in this, and to speak in this way is a useful shorthand method of stating a problem. However, if one looks at the situation through the eyes of the parents there is some reason to question the usefulness of this concept. Over and over again parents make the point that they feel they are no longer looked at or met in the normal way. This is both hurtful and the cause of much resentment. The fact that they have had a child with problems is certainly a very dominant one; but should it diminish in importance all their other qualities? Although rarely voiced, the cry can almost be heard – 'Yes, I have a handicapped child; yes, it has had a great effect on my whole way of life – but I am also still the person I was before, and *not* just a handicapped parent.' In the words of one father: 'We just want to be treated and listened to as *normal* people, not as handicapped people.'

Since such parents are already coping and, from the evidence, frequently unaided with the grief, shock, guilt feelings and practical implications of having such a child, it is unfortunate, to say the least, if they are also made to feel less of a person in their own right and in danger of losing their identity. This danger is increased at times because of the effects the birth of the handicapped child has had on relationships with spouse or partner, with family, friends and relations, with their other children and their way of life.

**Effects on Marital Relationships**

There is little doubt that having and caring for a handicapped child within the family increases the amount of stress. This stress is often felt most by the mother, who is most frequently the one who plays the greatest part in the day-to-day care, not only of the handicapped member, but also of the family as a whole.

The parents who responded to the questionnaire were asked specifically if their relations with their partners had been particularly affected. Interestingly nearly half of them reported no radical change, but of these slightly more than half felt that it had brought them closer together. They all reported their personal shock and grief on hearing the news and how fortunate they felt that they had been able to meet and share this together. A small number (approximately 12 per cent) did not reply to this section of questions at all but left it blank. There are several possible reasons for this; for instance, it might well have been that they felt the whole topic too painful to reply to; on the other hand, if there had been no effect they could have seen no reason to fill this in. All of the others reported changes which ranged from rejection of each other (sometimes leading to separation or divorce) to a great increase of care for each other and a closer, warmer relationship. 'We were both utterly shocked, but it brought us very close.'

This feeling of extra closeness and care for each other was reported by 15 per cent of the parents, in addition to the 25 per cent of those who had said that there was no radical change in their relationhip. However, this increased closeness within the relationship was frequently accompanied by a feeling of remoteness from their friends and the community at large:

> I think I cut myself off from friends and relations to a degree because I felt that they were embarrassed and distressed about the situation.

> The birth of my daughter completely changed our lives. We were thrown in upon ourselves. We never went out or visited or had visitors.

At the other extreme are the parents whose marriage completely broke down and ended in divorce or separation. Some of these parents do report however that the marriage was not satisfactory before. The birth of the handicapped child then proved to be the catalyst which brought matters to a head in one way or another:

> Her father could not come to terms with the fact that she was handicapped. Owing to the pressures, we just grew apart from each other.

> My husband didn't accept the situation; he blamed both himself and me at varying times. We were divorced when she was two and a half.

And in some ways perhaps the saddest of all the comments:

> Our marriage was not very good before she was born. Since then I have categorically refused to sleep with my husband.

Perhaps not surprisingly, it seems that the birth of a handicapped child does not fundamentally change the relationship, but it intensifies whatever the situation was previously, and in more ways than one this can be very destructive. More understanding on the part of relatives and friends and more easily obtained advice and consultation could well help to make life easier for the parents and possibly alleviate some of these consequences.

There are other consequences, one being that a number of the mothers are affected by feeling much more tied to the situation than their husband is: 'I resented the fact that my husband could get away during the day and I directed my frustrations at him when he came home.'

The mother of a child with cerebral palsy says: 'Because my child's needs were so demanding of me I became very aggressive to my husband.'

And the mother of a multiply handicapped child reports: 'I became extremely depressed and exhausted. My husband's way of coping was to escape, to pretend nothing was wrong. He stayed out far more.'

And another: 'There was an almost total lack of communication because I resented my husband's lack of support and involvement. We were two strangers living in the same house.'

A further matter of concern was the fact that in some cases the demanding needs of the child had a drastic effect upon the intimate marital relationship. Some of the mothers understood this but felt helpless to improve it:

> I had a great feeling of sadness for my husband, as he was not getting what he wanted. My life was devoted to looking after a sick child, and my husband's needs were not totally catered for.

> I felt it was my fault, and I was grateful that my husband still loved me. . . . Our lives were completely changed.

One mother of a cerebrally palsied child summed it up in this way: 'A handicapped child is like a drain. All your love, energy and money disappears down it with virtually no return, leaving little for anyone else.' Perhaps the words of this mother describe it best when she said: 'Having a handicapped child drew us together but kept us apart.'

It would be misleading not to report that a minority of the husbands showed their understanding and expressed their appreciation of the fact that the extra burden was being largely borne by their wives. One, for example, said: 'We felt it necessary to help each other and worked harder together.'

Many of the mothers commented on the support and help they got from their husbands. And one other father said: 'Undoubtedly many of the abilities and interests my daughter is developing have resulted from the untiring patience and perseverance of her mother.'

To sum up: the birth of a handicapped child does seem to have a deeper effect on the husband–wife relationship than the birth of a normal child, but the effect that it has is to intensify the relationship that previously existed. Where it is good it becomes deeper and more caring; where it is not good the extra stress can lead to 'living like two strangers under one roof' or to separation and divorce. Sometimes the increased closeness of the marital relationship can lead to a virtual shutting-down of other contacts, which may have destructive consequences. On the whole, the husbands in the survey seemed to find it more difficult than the wives either to accept the facts of the child's handicap or to come to terms with it. In some cases this led to them using avoidance techniques which added to the wives' burden and resulted in them developing feelings of frustration and aggression. On the other hand, some of the wives felt and acknowledged that they became almost totally absorbed by the demands made on them by the needs of the child, and that this had a detrimental effect on the time and care they could give to meeting their own needs and those of their husbands.

The main thing they all longed for, both husbands and wives, was a break from responsibility for a few hours and a chance to go out together. 'We never went out for a break for five and a half years' was an often repeated kind of comment. More than one study has demonstrated that the difference between a united or a divided family is directly related to the amount of relief from care that is available. Although the provision of relief care is still woefully inadequate, there is at least a growing awareness of the need, and different ways of meeting it are being devised. These will be discussed in Chapter 4.

## Effects on the Family

### *Siblings*

It is possibly true to say that the presence of a handicapped child in the family inevitably has some effect on the other children, but this will vary according to many things, such as the size of the family, the actual problems of the handicapped child and, most importantly, the attitudes of the parents and the extra demands that the necessary care of the handicapped child makes on the mother.

Some parents are determined to do their utmost to make sure the other children do not feel they have a duty to assume the responsibility of caring for their handicapped brother or sister when they are no longer able to do so. Others take the opposite view. This is a fundamental difference which determines the whole attitudes and practices of the family. It is very much a private and personal decision, and for those who expect the other members of the family to take over it is usually a very strongly held opinion. Often it is simply not open to discussion; in fact, it seems that such a discussion can be embarked upon only if it is opened by a member of the family. The parents who hold the contrary view are equally firm in their conviction but are much more prepared to discuss the whole subject. They also feel that if, when they are of an age and in a position to make the decision of their own free will, another member of the family does decide to assume the care and responsibility then this is a totally different situation and one that is acceptable. The avoidance of any sort of pressure is their main concern.

Even though many parents reported that, for example, 'We live in a volatile, highly charged atmosphere due to the disturbed child', one of the chief concerns of them all is to maintain as much normality as possible in the other children's lives. One of the main difficulties in achieving this is, of course, the sheer amount of time, energy and care that has to be given in many cases to the handicapped child. Over and over again it was said, 'We had less time to spend with our other children', or 'We couldn't do much as a family.'

The position of the child in the family also has an effect. A typical example of the consequences of the handicapped child being the eldest was described by one parent as follows: 'My youngest child never really knew what it was like to be a baby; the middle child had all the disadvantages of being the eldest and none of the privileges.'

Older siblings are often thrust into a position of responsibility in spite of the parents' wish to avoid this, and this has different consequences. One mother whose husband was very supportive and loving reported that her older normal son learned 'to have empathy with other people's children'.

Sometimes the whole family developed the feeling that 'We had a job to do as a family; sharing this drew us together.' One mother reported: 'I felt my older daughter was neglected and so over-compensated in other directions.' Another was concerned because 'my elder daughter was expected to make allowances for her mentally handicapped brother, and responsibility was thrust upon her.'

Many parents worrying 'about our other children missing out in some ways' did try to alleviate this: 'I tried not to make them feel they were obliged to look after her when they wanted to go out to play, for instance, but I found that their relationship with her grew over the years and *it came from them*.'

The outcome was not always so happy:

> My son got far less attention because of profound difficulties with my multiply handicapped daughter. He was three when she was born, but not really jealous till she started to make progress when he was seven. From three to seven he did miss out on parental attention, but subsequently he has had his share, and more, we hope.

There is a high possibility that a child having such experiences in his or her early childhood will subsequently develop psychological difficulties.

Many other examples could be quoted. Sometimes, as has been shown, the outcome is positive, but in other cases having a handicapped sibling has clearly been a difficult, or even harmful, experience for children to cope with, especially when very young. The knowledge of this can increase mothers' concern and stress, particularly because they often feel unable to do anything positive about it: 'My other children had to take a back seat, which concerned me as they had only just started school themselves.'

One of the saddest examples was that of a family of three boys, two of whom were handicapped; the normal child was the middle one, and the parents said:

> We think sometimes that he is the one who is most affected. He has no obvious handicap, but has very much a handicap in having a handicapped brother on either side. He has never been able to talk to his brothers, or even fight or discuss things with them. He has always to be caring, protective and very often embarrassed.

Other consequences are that the family sometimes has to be split up, for example: 'My older daughter was looked after almost exclusively by my mother until she was two and we had to move away. My younger daughter was considerably neglected, about which she is still very bitter.' The problem is exacerbated if the handicapped child needs constant medical care and attention. The father of a rubella-damaged child became very ill: 'My older child became very grown up very quickly; he became very nervous and he became ill.'

Often there are financial problems. The mother may have been working and so has either to stop work or to pay for someone else to do the caring. A study of 303 families with severely disturbed children showed that, compared with a control group, the fathers' incomes were generally lower, and the mothers' substantially so. These deficiencies were not made good by benefits paid on account of the child's disability.[1]

One of the saddest consequences for siblings can arise from the attitudes and prejudices of other children and their families. This can limit and sometimes destroy their social life – this is apart from the tendency already mentioned that some of the parents have to withdraw from social contacts. For example, one mother reported that her daughters had difficulties in bringing friends home, but this was mainly because of the attitudes of their parents. Another was bitterly hurt when she received a note saying that if the note-writer's daughter came to visit and brought toys would she please make sure that the handicapped child did not play with them. It may well have been that the note-sending mother did not want the toys to be soiled or broken. But there were other ways of safeguarding this without causing extra hurt, through lack of tact and sensitivity, to a parent already dealing with many difficulties, including perhaps (for some mothers acknowledge this) feelings of jealousy because the other mother had no handicapped child.

To sum up: the relationship of parents of a handicapped child with their normal children is subject to many strains. Most parents are aware of this, however, and sometimes at much extra cost to themselves, do all that they can to keep the situation as normal as possible. The children are no less vulnerable as a result, but many not only survive the experience but, in the long run, become more caring and understanding of other people's problems because of it. The one thing no parent in the survey said was that they regretted having had more children, in spite of all the extra work, anxieties and responsibilities they brought.

**Effects on Relationships in the Extended Family and with Friends**

In one sense the use of the phrase 'extended family' is misleading, since the extended family in modern Western society has on the whole given way to the nuclear family. It is all too rarely the case nowadays that different members of a family live near to each other, and in consequence the news of the birth of a handicapped child in the family can have far less impact on grandparents and other relatives than it had in previous times. Very often too grandparents are still actively working and far less free to be involved in helping.

It may be partly for this reason that some grandparents seem to be unwilling or unable to accept the full extent of a child's handicaps and the problems of the parents. They express sympathy and shock but can go on to say, as did the parents of the mother of a child with cerebral palsy, 'Oh, he's just a bit slower than normal. He'll be OK.'

Sometimes parents find themselves in the position of 'cushioning the disappointment' and reassuring the family instead of receiving the help they would have liked: 'We were given sympathy, but help – no.' Some more fortunate did get help and support, but this was mentioned very infrequently. Others experienced resentment and rejection mainly of the child, a good example of this being the following case: 'Some relations ignore the fact that he exists. They send our other boys presents, cards, money, but nothing is ever sent for him. This really hurts.'

In general the effect on relationships with friends and contemporaries was much more frequently commented upon than relationships with family. Grandparents' or other relatives' reactions were often dismissed in a few words, generally 'They were sad' or 'No change.'

Relationships with friends were affected in two different ways. Some became closer, while others almost ceased to exist: 'Our friends stopped calling.' This was sometimes because of the reactions of the friends, but more frequently it was the parents who for one reason or another ceased to develop or continue the relationship. There was some evidence that the degree of closeness with the friends before the child was born had an effect; for instance, one mother said: 'Our close friends became even closer. The casual acquaintances kept away – the invitations stopped coming, which really hurt.'

Another mother made an allied point: 'Invitations do not usually include the handicapped child.' Another said: 'We relied heavily on old friends but developed a carefulness about making new friends.'

The reason most commonly given for withdrawing from friendships was 'lack of time'. For example: 'Most of my time was taken up by my child. I could have no social life at all.' Many felt that it was difficult enough to cope with the needs and demands of the handicapped child and to give some time and attention to the rest of the family and the chores of everyday life. They had no time or energy left for anything else, while at the same time wishing to have other contacts: 'We had less time for our other daughter and each other. Social life and general relationships with friends were adversely affected.'

There were other reasons given, for instance: 'I think I cut myself off from friends and relations to a degree because I felt they were embarrassed and distressed about the situation' – although there was no evidence from the friends that this was the case. It may well have stemmed from the parents' own conflict about the situation, as seems to be more clearly the case in this example: 'We couldn't tell our friends for more than four months. We felt we had to keep it to ourselves.'

Conflict was caused between a husband and wife in another instance because the wife feared the reactions of her friends and relations, while the husband could not agree with her about that or her wish to withdraw because of it. Other mothers honestly faced the fact that it was their own feelings of jealousy and anger that caused the problem: 'I found it very difficult to be with my friends, especially those with normal children of the same age, because of my jealousy and other emotions.' This mother stressed that it was not in any way her friends' fault but all due to her own feelings.

Another significant reason was the embarrassment parents felt because of the bizarre or destructive behaviour of their child, especially when out of their own home. Such embarrassment was not helped by the unkind or unthinking comments sometimes made by bystanders: 'As it was a nightmare taking my child anywhere, I stayed at home and did not make friends or cultivate existing friends. I became very introverted.'

Even well-meaning but tactless remarks have to be endured sometimes; for example, one mother taking her Down's syndrome baby for a walk was accosted by a stranger with the remark, 'Oh, you poor dear – weren't you warned that this could happen at your age?' The irony of this particular case was that the baby was in fact adopted; his own parents had not felt able to accept him and he had first been fostered and then adopted. It did make it easier for the mother to deal with the comment emotionally, but it does not take much imagination to see how a natural mother would react to a remark of that kind.

There is frequently another complication which occurs when parents join a group or society and become involved in some way with mutual activities with other parents whose children have the same handicap. It is partly because this is often very helpful in many ways that parents come to feel obliged to spend what little free time they have available helping in the work of the society, and so their life becomes almost a closed circle of handicap from which they feel there is no escape. The one thing that all the parents in the survey with very few exceptions said they felt most in need of was a 'holiday' or 'a rest from responsibilities'; 'If only my husband and I could sometimes go out together'; or most poignantly, 'If only I could have one undisturbed night's sleep.'

Putting on one side all the emotional and humanitarian reasons for making this possible, there is a hard-headed and practical reason for it also. Every child or handicapped person living at home is costing the state far less than any other form of provision would entail. Relatively inexpensive measures which have already been initiated in some places by parent groups, societies and local authorities could give all parents who wished for it some chance of relief and the opportunity to give more time to each other, their other children, their friends, their hobbies and interests. Such arrangements would also save some from breaking down under the strain. These will be discussed in Chapter 4.

## Notes

1. Baldwin and others, 'Childhood disabilities and family income', *Journal of Epidemiology and Community Health*, vol. 37, no. 3, pp 167–95.

CHAPTER 4

# Meeting Parents' Needs

## Parents Talking

Basically I needed help in convincing professionals that I did have a special child.

Friends find him so difficult. I never asked them to 'baby-sit' a second time. *I* needed them to talk to.

We needed just to be treated and listened to as normal people.

I soon realised that anything I wanted done for my daughter would have to be done by me.

Health visitors, social workers and such visit and promise lots of help, but that's how it stops – a promise.

There were some wires pulling me one way and *one* pulling the other.

I would have liked people to recognise my child's potential and *listen* to me, and I deeply resented having my child referred to as a 'case study'.

My wonderful baby-sitter has kept me sane through all this. Official sources of help are fairly useless. A social worker came a couple of times – she got more depressed than I did.

If we are willing to cope at home most of the time, why is there no nursing *at home* available when we need a break? Baby-sitting from a competent person at all stages would have been the biggest help, as we could then have had time for a little life of our own.

I would like to have been given some type of structured programme with goals to work towards whereby we would have felt we were doing something to help the child.

> Because like so many of these children she screamed a lot and slept very little, there was always tiredness and the pressure of friends and relations looking for us to give in, in some way or another.

**Parents' Needs**

In this book so far the problems and stresses felt and experienced by the parents and families of handicapped children in the early years have been described. It is clear that the parents have certain needs which, though relatively simple, are often ignored or neglected. Briefly, they are as follows:

- The need for support and reassurance.
- The need for practical help.
- The need for information.
- The need for 'someone to talk to'.
- The need to be shown that they are still regarded as someone in their own right and not just the parent of a handicapped child.
- The need to have some time for a 'break' and temporary relief from the perpetual demands and responsibilities.
- The need for the husband and wife or partners to have some time together and to enjoy some purely social contacts.
- The need to be shown how to do something positive to help their child.

To some extent some of these needs have already been discussed. Communication between the parents and those who should be dealing with them, although extremely important, is often unsatisfactory. There seems to be a great lack of understanding by all concerned of the best way to approach each other. To give a simple example of this, a doctor or nurse fully familiar with medical terminology may well not realise how unfamiliar the parents and other lay people may be with those terms. There can therefore be genuine misunderstanding on this verbal level.

At least as important is the lack of understanding on the emotional level. By their training and the nature of their work, doctors have to acquire and practise professional detachment. This is all too easily seen as coldness or lack of sympathy by the parents. Hopefully, as more medical education courses are developed dealing with the problems of communication this will improve. Meanwhile there seems to be a need and place for a sympathetic person who is also knowledgeable and who can supplement and expand upon the information given by the doctor.

A further point has been made by the doctors, and that is that frequently parents and patients approach them at a time or in a way that is inappropriate. With the best will in the world a doctor with a full waiting-room of other patients, or just about to go out to make home visits, or to go to an emergency, cannot take the time to listen to or to discuss a problem which has no immediate urgency, important though it undoubtedly is to the person wishing to raise it. The doctors do appreciate that anxiety is frequently the cause of this wish and would willingly do what they could if asked when the time was more favourable. Unfortunately an apparent rejection can lead to a long-lasting misunderstanding.

Here again, a sympathetic person who has the confidence of the parents could be invaluable. This role could be undertaken by a variety of people; a health visitor or a social worker is the obvious professional who could be involved. There are, however, various reasons why they are not always the best person to undertake the task. At the present time they both inevitably carry a large case-load and in consequence cannot always give as much time to any one case as either they or the client would like. In addition, they have established professional roles. The role of the health visitor is to visit, to assess a need and then to pass on the information to those who should supply it; only in exceptional circumstances can he or she undertake to do more. Perhaps a stronger case can be made for expecting more of the social worker, but except in cases of emergency they literally do not have time to do more than make periodic visits to see that all appears to be going well.

There also frequently seems to be a communication problem between a number of the parents and the social worker who is allotted to them, if in fact one is. There is evidence of this in many reports, as for example in the Action Research report *They get this training but they don't really know how you feel* (see note 1, page 13), and in the accounts of individual cases where, sadly, things have gone wrong.

Many parents made the same point in their answers to the questionnaire. One mother summed up the feelings and experiences of many when she wrote:

> The help you get or even get offered is very much dependent on whom you have dealings with. Over and over again throughout our daughter's life the people who are in contact with you are not experienced enough in the needs of a handicapped person or the problems the families suffer, i.e. social workers, health visitors, doctors. Also, getting these people to take note of what you say instead of the normal pattern of answers you receive, such as 'things must be hard' or 'things must be getting on top of you' or 'your emotions are confused' or 'there is no answer to that'.

This last may be true, as is also the honest, 'I don't know' – honest, but not satisfactory if it is left at that, because the question immediately arises as to why a professional person does not know the answer to a practical question, or at least does not offer to find out what the answer is. The trouble is that no matter how well meaning these comments are they sound to the listener very shallow, glib and unthinking. It would be wrong to give the impression that there are no health visitors or social workers who meet the needs of their clients; many do their work admirably and are valued by the people they help. Yet this appears to depend on the personality of the professional and, more importantly perhaps, on their ability to convey to anxious parents the concern which many of them undoubtedly feel. One mother gave one answer when she wrote: 'The task of dealing with parents in such situations should be given to *experienced* professionals, and not recently trained professionals. Perhaps it would be useful to evaluate the relationships between professionals and clients in emotional rather than purely clinical terms.'

Recently the situation appears to have improved, at least for the parents of the mentally handicapped wherever there are community nurses functioning. This may be due to the fact that they are not having to deal with a multiplicity of functions, as are the social workers for instance. Again, some authorities are beginning to meet the need for information by using pamphlets or booklets which are given to the parents of known children with special needs explaining the services available and giving some information as to who should be approached if these services are required. It would be possible to extend this idea and to devise a suitable booklet to be given to the parents whenever a child found to be handicapped is born, or when diagnosis has been made. Such a booklet should explain simply the child's handicap and tell the parents who they can go to to get more information both about the problem and about what can be done to help. The point has already been made that parents do not always assimilate the information they receive when they are still in the state of shock they all experience when first hearing the news; however, if they were to be given such a booklet they could refer to it when they felt ready to do so and act accordingly.

**Someone to Talk to**

On all the available evidence the need for someone to talk to is one of the most commonly felt needs. Baffled, frightened, lonely and insecure, parents long for, as one parent put it, 'a sympathetic ear'. Many suggested that the person they would welcome most would be someone who had had a similar experience.

Some ways of meeting this need have already been discussed in this book, as for example the work of the Southend Group (Chapter 2). Out of this same need many parents' and mutual aid associations have been set up. Some have grown into large societies, such as MENCAP and the Spastics Society. Others which tend to be smaller are allied to specific handicaps. Personal contact between the parents is much more easily achieved within the larger associations, since local groups can be formed from their members and also more specialised groups may be allied to the parent body, as for instance the Down's Children's Association. These societies and associations were all set up originally by the drive and energy of parents who, feeling a need strongly, worked actively to supply it; they do invaluable work and are constantly growing as new developments take place. Admirable though their work is, it does make further demands on the parents, on the whole willingly undertaken it is true; but there is a case for examining this whole area, to see if it is not possible to give the parents more help in running these activities.

There are other problems which can be associated with this way of giving help and support – some of which are discussed in the book *Self-Help and Social Care*.[1] One of the most commonly found problems is the apparent apathy of the majority of the members and their unwillingness to play an active role in the group. In consequence the whole work tends to depend on the few members who are willing and free to do it, and problems arise when one of them has to be replaced. There are other members who, while wishing to support the society, do not feel that they can offer help to others. They joined to get help and, when their own need is past, find that the years of dealing with the problem have left them unwilling to prolong the period of being associated with it; they just want to relax and to enjoy the relief of being free. Fortunately – because there is no doubt of the value of these organisations – there are invariably a few people willing to act as leaders and advisers. What is lacking in many cases is sufficient training and support for these leaders. Again, this seems to be an area where more could be done to help.

### *The Need for Reassurance*

Parents of handicapped children often mention the need to be shown that they are still people in their own right.

> We needed just to be treated and listened to as normal people and not as handicapped people.

> We feel that there is a habit of treating parents as patients with a disease of which the children are symptoms.

These comments are typical examples of a deeply felt emotion experienced by many parents of handicapped children. It is probable that in many cases the feeling of being treated as someone apart comes, at least partly, from within the parents themselves. Their own emotional turmoil has made them super-sensitive. Whereas, if their baby had been normal, they would have been able to accept the somewhat maternalistically superior manner of address adopted by some professionals, they are unable to do this in the circumstances. Other parents comment on the fact that sometimes it feels to them as if the professionals are embarrassed about the whole situation and therefore cannot adopt a normal way of dealing with them.

Even more important to the parents, however, is the fact that this same attitude seems to affect their friends and the other people they regularly come in contact with. This is difficult to deal with, reflecting as it does our society's attitude to handicap. Very few people seem to have the ability of knowing how to deal with it when they meet it in their own circle, and hence tend either to be emotionally sympathetic to excess, or to opt out of the situation.

They either never refer to it or withdraw from the contact. For the past few generations we have avoided contact with handicapped people, and this perhaps applies especially to the mentally handicapped. Society's answer to the problem has been to deem it necessary to remove them to be cared for in secure institutions. There has even been an element of fear connected with this.

Attitudes and policies are changing now, but it will take some time for these changes to be generally accepted. It should not be forgotten that in many respects the parents are experiencing many of the same emotions that outsiders feel, and so find it difficult to indicate to other people the reaction they would like to meet. The situation will not be improved either if, in our wish to give community acceptance to handicapped people, we 'gloss over' the fact that the handicap exists; for this is another false attitude which can lead only to disillusion. It is not a situation which can be dealt with in general solutions. All that can be done is to draw attention to the facts and hope that the more that is known about the situation, the easier it will become for everyone to deal with it.

**The Need for a 'Break': Respite Care**

It is generally believed that the present policy of caring for the handicapped within the community and, if possible, within their own family is correct. However, the implementing of this policy does not seem to have been totally thought out, the amount of strain it can put upon a family not fully appreciated. Many things have been improved, not least the education service now available, and particularly the fact that it can start at a very early age. Medical care has improved, and aids and equipment are now provided for use in the home, although unfortunately parents do not always know that they are entitled to them, or how to get them. This even applies to such simple but fundamental necessities as incontinence pads. This is all part of the communication problem, as already discussed.

To return to the positive side, the attendance allowance has helped to ease the financial burden, and when in August 1983 it became possible for parents to continue to claim it for up to four weeks when the handicapped person was in short-term residential care, one reason for some parents refusing to take advantage of such provision if they were offered it, much though they felt the need for it, was removed.

The one provision that was acknowledged to be essential – relief and support for the care-givers – appears to be the one that is slowest to be provided in adequate measure. There are reasons for this, many of them concerned with the legal aspects of providing respite and short-term care. There is no one clear-cut legislative framework under which it can operate, and therefore different problems arise according to which section of the law those wishing to make such provision choose to operate under. Questions regarding such matters as insurance cover and legal responsibility are important and have to be agreed. Relief care workers need training and advice if a scheme is to be operated successfully, and there is, as yet, no recognised training programme. Many authorities wishing to set up one of these schemes do however ensure that some training is provided within their own resources. But, as do the parents, relief care workers also need support. These are just some of the issues which are having to be resolved at the same time as attempts are being made to provide the services.

Services are offered by different agencies. Some are provided by the statutory services, i.e. the social services, health and education authorities; others by voluntary societies as, for example, the Church of England's Children's Society, Dr Barnardo's and similar bodies; and some also by groups of parents banding together for the purpose. Sometimes a combination of these services provides the best service. For instance, children may be regularly admitted for short-term care to a children's home run by a voluntary body, with the cost met by social services. Ideally a range of provision should be available so that parents can choose the arrangements they feel to be most appropriate, but this ideal is very rarely possible at present. Parents have either to accept whatever is available, to do without or to make their own arrangements.

### *Types of Respite Care*

There are four main types of respite care:

- Residential care.
- Family-based care.
- Care in the child's own home.
- Holiday schemes.

Each scheme offers parents the time off they so desperately need and each has advantages and disadvantages. If, however, they were all available (and at present this is far from being the case) the parents would be able to choose the one they felt would best suit their child's and their own needs at any particular time, since this will obviously vary.

### *Residential Care*

Residential care offers parents the possibility of periodic relief, when the child or older handicapped member of the family goes to stay for whatever period is agreed upon in approved accommodation. This accommodation is usually provided in an institution of some kind, but this can vary from a bed on a hospital ward to a boarding place in a child's own school, a bed in a children's home or unit, or a hostel. The disadvantage of this type of provision is that it is 'institution' based, and many parents are reluctant to use it for this reason. This particularly applies to hospital provision, where the bed available might be in a paediatric ward, a general hospital ward or a ward in a mental handicap hospital. Whichever it is, the problem is that the way of life provided is in complete contrast to the pattern of life at home with the family. This still applies even though life in a hospital these days has been vastly improved. The same is true, although to a much lesser degree, of a stay in a children's home, hostel or school.

The great advantage of this type of care is that it can offer respite from the most handicapped as well as those less affected and also in a consistent way which will become familiar to the children and the family over a period of time. Even though some staff may change from time to time, the pattern remains consistent. Once accepted by the parents, they can enjoy the relief it offers with far less anxiety because it is not dependent upon one family or person being able to continue to offer the service. Normally it is also a service which is free.

### *Family-Based Care*

This is an expanding type of respite care which formally began in Leeds and Somerset in 1975 and is now being made available in other areas. It applies to families with a handicapped child. Such a family is linked with a family who is willing and able to take the handicapped child into its home for whatever period of time, and as often as, is needed.

Such schemes are usually promoted and managed by one of the statutory services, usually social services. A typical example of such a scheme was set up in 1984 by a borough in the Home Counties. The scheme was initiated by a publicity campaign and the appointment of a part-time social worker to manage and organise it. As a result of the publicity and the meetings which followed it some prospective families were found. The word 'families' is slightly misleading, because single people are welcome to take part in the scheme. The aim is to offer short-term care in a local family for any child or young person, mentally or physically handicapped, living in the borough, up to the age of nineteen.

It was decided that the respite offered should be for periods ranging from a few hours to a maximum of two weeks. The relief parents are paid on a sessional basis by the Social Services Department. However, the parents using the scheme are asked to pay a small contribution if they can afford it. They do not pay the relief parents directly but buy a book of vouchers from the social worker and give the relief parent a voucher for every session they use the service. The relief parents are all given an initial period of training, and it is arranged that the families meet each other. The service starts only when both sets of parents have accepted each other and the child has accepted the relief parent. From then on, although the social worker is kept informed and can be contacted if the need arises, all arrangements are made between the families. Before the scheme comes into operation the social worker draws up an agreement with both sets of parents stating clearly what arrangements will be made regarding visits, timing of visits, what equipment the parents will provide, transport arrangements and so on. This is essential if potential sources of disagreement are to be avoided. When the child actually starts the visits the relief parent is given a detailed fact sheet compiled by the social worker detailing the child's special needs, medical situation, problems, likes, dislikes, drugs, routines, etc. This fact sheet will accompany the child on every visit.

The scheme is now working with several families and appears to be going well. Similar schemes are to be found in several other localities.

This type of family relief scheme has obvious advantages. The parents get the breaks they need, normally as they feel the need for them. The child has an extended social experience while at the same time being in familiar surroundings and able to continue to attend his or her own school in the usual way. However, some criticisms have been voiced, largely on the grounds that many of the presumed benefits, particularly to the child, are at present based only on assumptions. It is felt that possibly the whole approach may have been accepted in too uncritical a way, and that it is essential that research should be carried out to evaluate the efficiency and value of such schemes. There is also a fear that because this type of respite is relatively inexpensive it may well be used when other forms of relief would be more appropriate.

### *Care in the Child's Own Home*

This type of care is, in essence, a specialised form of 'baby-sitting' and has many advantages for the child who needs specialised equipment or who becomes distressed when being cared for away from their own home. It also offers the opportunity to become relief parents to people who, for one reason or another, could not take a child into their own home. In some areas peripatetic care workers are used, and such a scheme can also form part of an extended home-help service. However, unlike the usual pattern of home help the helper is there to take over the care of the child and not to do the domestic chores. If this type of service is developed, the preparation for it to be started needs to be very similar to that described for the family-based scheme described above.

## Holiday Schemes

There are holiday schemes available for children with special needs. Some provide for the children only, others for the whole family. They are usually seen as an additional part of respite care and provide a very useful service.

They are organised by a variety of agencies and take many forms. One problem is that they normally have to be paid for, and since we are in a period of financial stringency the necessary funding often has to be provided by the parents. This is not through lack of goodwill on the part of the social services or other statutory bodies but simply that there is not enough money available. There are some voluntary bodies which do help, such as the Rowntree Trust, which also offers most generous assistance in many other ways.

The need for parents and other carers to have some breaks from the constant demands of looking after any handicapped member of the family is now generally accepted, and appropriate means of providing it can now be found in many parts of the country. Suitable provision is not always available, however. Many parents feel very reluctant to accept some form of institutional care as a 'holiday' placement. The private schemes are usually very good but they are not cheap (for one thing, a high staff ratio is required); so some parents frequently do without.

One wonders whether the necessary funding should have to depend so much on the parents or on charitable help. Consideration could and should be given to providing such services on a different, more professional basis. More family-type hostels would ease the situation greatly, particularly if parents were assured that a bed would be regularly available for their use. If a part of the time of the staff of these hostels was devoted to 'home care' and visiting families, then the situation would be without stress for all using it, and the parents would use the service with an easy mind. Extending the idea, hostels could be 'twinned' with hostels in other areas to make holiday exchange visits possible. There would still be a place for, and a great need of, voluntary help, but the main structure would be stable and consistent and, probably once the initial period of setting-up had been paid for, no more expensive than the present random provision.

There is also one further point in favour of such a scheme; it would not have the 'cut-off' point which at present operates in many of the existing provisions at about the age of nineteen. The problems and handicaps still exist, but the child is no longer a child, and it is far more difficult to consider providing family relief services for someone who has physically become an adult. There is nothing strikingly original about this plan; lip-service is always being paid to the desirability of providing hostels, and many agencies would willingly set about doing it. The only things required are the necessary drive, will and, most important of all, the necessary funds.

## Other Forms of Support

There are some associations, mainly charities, which exist to complement and assist the work done by the statutory services. One of the most active of these is known as Contact a Family.[2]

*Contact a Family*

The main aim of this association is to contact the families who have a handicapped member and then actively to set about helping them. The organisation has various projects in London and also in the South and West of the country, working mainly in inner-city or neglected rural areas. Each local project is run by a co-ordinator, most of whom are trained volunteers working under the overall guidance and support of a support and liaison personnel officer, who is based at Contact a Family's central office. Briefly, the task of each co-ordinator is:

- To form the link with statutory and voluntary agencies.
- To find and contact families by such means as visiting special schools and discussing with social workers, health visitors and paediatricians.
- To help set up a neighbourhood group where families can meet together in a social way and also exchange experiences and share their problems.
- To maintain and give continuing support to the group once it has been established.
- To co-ordinate and develop ideas and activities with the families.
- To provide information and resources.
- To support, train and supervise the Contact a Family workers.

A full and comprehensive task!

The Contact a Family workers, who are all volunteers, maintain the services offered, acting for example as baby-sitters and volunteer drivers, helping with shopping and also with recreational activities such as swimming, riding and holiday schemes. One of the most valuable and interesting features of the organisation is the way it involves unemployed and young people in the work undertaken. Another is the fact that the siblings of the handicapped are not ignored but included in the outings and social activities. Attempts are made to meet their needs as well as those of the handicapped member. Other organisations also participate in their activities, such as the Red Cross, youth clubs, Cubs and Townswomen's Guild. All these features distinguish the Contact a Family groups from the mutual aid ones and are truly based on community involvement and care.

**Cope**

In this chapter it has not been possible to cover all the services that exist to bring help and support to the families in need of them. Those which have been described are given as examples of what is being attempted. Although many efforts are being made, it would be wrong to give the impression that those which exist are sufficient to meet the demand. At best they show what can be done, but even if there were sufficient resources available to make provision for all there would still be some parents who either could not or would not make use of them. It is this problem that COPE is designed to deal with by means of its family groups.[3]

COPE is an independent national voluntary organisation which exists to promote the development of groups for families with problems. It does not run projects directly but is designed to help statutory and voluntary groups throughout Britain which do. It is funded by the DHSS and several charitable foundations. Its main purpose is to promote family groups as a means of providing education and social care in the community, and of doing preventive work. These family groups are small and informal neighbourhood groups of people who meet regularly for mutual support, encouragement and enjoyment. They are outside the statutory services of all agencies, but have the backing and support of health, education, social and community services. They are not intended solely for the parents of the handicapped but to help all those people who are isolated within a community and lacking in the confidence and social skills which would enable them to take advantage of the services available. These include people who are depressed or preoccupied with problems such as unemployment, poor housing and too many small children. Among them can be found some parents of children with special needs. These groups are led by people recruited from the local community, the team usually consisting of a leader, play-leader and assistant play-leader. They are paid by the session and after selection undergo a preparation course.

People who may need them are usually invited into a group normally by the leader, although some are referred by social workers. Since the emphasis in these groups is on social activities they manage to attract people who are hostile to, or suspicious of, the official services. They usually meet once a week and often join in some shared activity. Most importantly they provide the opportunity for social intercourse, and through having been a member of such a group people frequently develop the confidence to go on to accept what society has to offer in the way of relief and support for their particular problems.

## Developmental Goals: The Portage Project

There is one final need felt by parents to be discussed, and that is the wish they have to be advised how to help their child. They want to be doing something positive and not to appear to be passively accepting the finality of the problem. Actively doing something also eases to some degree their own hurt. Some feel so strongly about this that they are not prepared to accept a medical opinion that there is little that they can usefully do. To some extent this determination has led to many advances and changes of opinion. At the very least it has brought about a reappraisal of long-held convictions. An example of this is the finding that hyperactivity, previously assumed to be the consequence of minimal cerebral dysfunction, can be caused by food allergies due mainly to food additives. Down's children are no longer automatically assumed to be incapable of learning. Autistic children are being improved, and much is being learned by the attempts to improve their condition. Many other examples could be given.

One thing that is becoming generally accepted is that, whatever the handicap, early stimulation is vitally important, and that in nearly all cases the earlier the correct intervention takes place the greater the improvements that can be expected. It has been for some time the practice for specialist teachers and other advisers to visit the parents of severely visually and auditorally handicapped children in their homes to give advice and help from a very early age on the teaching and management of their child and also on the facilities that are available to benefit both themselves and their child. This service is now being extended to children with other special needs. This is partly because it is becoming the established pattern that a child's potential is no longer assessed from the clinical diagnosis of his or her condition but rather it is analysed from what the child can do, what is desirable for him or her to do next and what is needed to achieve this aim. The most widely used and structured use of this technique is known as the Portage Project.

### *The Portage Project*

This project is so named because it was first developed in Portage, Wisconsin, USA, in 1969.[4] It was introduced into the UK in 1976. Portage is a home-based intervention programme, intended to be used from immediately after birth to mental age six. Although it was originally designed for use with mentally handicapped children it is now known to be equally valuable for children with many other types of handicap. It is a complex service which offers a structured teaching programme, largely carried out by the parents, but with the co-operation of a home teacher who regularly visits and offers support to the parents.

The Portage schemes are usually set up and supervised by the Schools' Psychological Service, and the home teachers are trained by the psychologist responsible in that area. The teachers are recruited from other disciplines and add the home teaching to their regular work pattern. This is now altering since the Department of Education and Science laid down a structure which from April 1986 made provision for full-time Portage teachers. A typical team of home teachers in one area included health visitors, speech and physiotherapists, a social worker and a teacher, some of whom already visited the family they were assigned to in their other capacity. As part of their contract they were required to attend regular supervision meetings, which were in fact very supportive to the teachers, since they offered the opportunity for passing on the experience gained and for discussion of any difficulties, plus realistic future planning.

Portage offers the parents taking part in the scheme a completely unique assessment of their child, taking place in their own home, and with them involved as a partner, not a client. Indeed, it has been claimed that Portage is part of the reaction now taking place to the habit of treating parents as patients. Together, each week, the parents and the teacher select an educational goal to be worked towards during the next week. This will be carried out by the parents according to the methods suggested by the teacher. The result is checked and assessed the following week, and a new target decided upon. Throughout the time the parent keeps a regular record and progress chart and is loaned any material that may be required to meet the target set.

Portage also is a means of introducing the parents to the most advanced teaching procedures devised and tested for children with special needs. It has other values too, one of the chief being that it eliminates completely the parents' feelings of isolation and of being left alone to struggle with their many problems. It is frequently the case that the visiting home teacher becomes the mother's confidant and 'listening ear' with whom she feels able to discuss some of her many anxieties. Among the topics reported to have been talked about in this way are the attitudes of families and friends, the effect on the rest of the family, genetic counselling, thoughts of death and of infanticide, attitudes of the medical profession and anxieties about the future. If the teacher does not feel able to handle these subjects adequately, the fact that the mother has been able to voice them is still very important, and among other benefits it allows the teacher to suggest to the mother someone who can give her adequate help.

The goals set fall into five different areas, and it is an important part of the planning which area should be chosen for the immediate target. The areas are: (1) motor skills, (2) social development, (3) language development, (4) cognitive learning and (5) self-help skills. The choice is determined by the child's needs plus the emphasis the parent places on different skills, since the child will get most benefit if the parent teaching him or her believes in the importance of that skill. Evaluation in different parts of the country has demonstrated that the children learn on average seven new skills a month. Home-based Portage normally stops when the child goes to school. It has been shown that a child who has been helped with Portage starts school on an improved basis because of the skills he or she has attained, and that the parents, through what they have learned, usually have a much greater appreciation of what the school is attempting to do.

Portage has much to offer, but it does not succeed with all children. Questions are being raised as to why this is so, and also whether, as with respite care, too much is being assumed to be good without it having been established by research that it is so. One criticism of Portage is that problems can arise as a result of the emphasis given by the project to specific immediate gains (the attainment of weekly goals) at the expense of long-term objectives.

This is exemplified in language development, where the criticism has been made that Portage aims fail to give enough practice in the use of language in real situations, and therefore the language skills attained are not generalised.

It has been shown that family and child variables have a great effect on the success, or lack of it, in the Portage Project. Some children do better if, in place of Portage, they are visited regularly by the health visitor plus some pre-school attendance at play-groups, or developmental classes, where these exist. Another suggestion is that the main advantage of Portage is the effect it has on the parents' morale, because the very fact that intervention is taking place conveys to them the message that the child is capable of learning. This in turn gives them hope for the future, so their whole approach to the child becomes more positive. This seems to be another instance where the ideal would be to have both alternatives – Portage and pre-school activities – available so that parents could choose which they preferred or even use a mixture of the two.

What has been established beyond doubt is that intervention of the one kind or the other, plus parent support, is far more effective than no support in terms of the child's rate of development and parental satisfaction. Whatever may be said, Portage is a technique which can be adapted to help many children with differing special needs. It is now commonly used in a much more flexible manner than when it was first introduced. In many cases it has been adapted so that workers take from it whatever they feel is most appropriate to help the children and parents they are working with.

### *Other Approaches*

Other parents concentrate their energies and efforts on techniques which they feel are more appropriate to deal with the particular needs of their child. A striking example of this are those parents who undertake the exhausting and demanding techniques initiated by the Institute for the Achievement of Human Potential in Philadelphia to help children with severe brain damage. These involve constant body manipulation and virtually take over the whole pattern of life for the family, who also need to enlist the help of a team of friends and supporters to maintain the activities without a break in their regularity. To call it a superhuman task is an understatement; nevertheless parents do undertake it and are encouraged by the results they achieve. These techniques have been subject to much criticism and are controversial, but the point being made is that whatever techniques they choose to use the pain of the parents is being alleviated to some extent by the fact that they are doing something positive to help their child, and the child is being given stimulation. This can only be beneficial.

## Notes

1. Ann Richardson and Meg Goodman, *Self-Help and Social Care*, Mutual Aid Organisations in Practice No. 612, London, Policy Studies Institute, May 1983.
2. Reports and leaflets from Contact a Family, 16 Strutton Ground, Victoria, London SW1P 2HP.
3. Information and pamphlets from COPE, 19–29 Woburn Place, London WC1H 0LY.
4. Suggested further reading on Portage: Tony Dessent (ed.), *What Is Important about Portage?* Proceedings of the 1982 National Conference on Portage Services, Slough, NFER/Nelson, April 1984; B. Daley (ed.) et al., *Portage: The Importance of Parents*, Slough, NFER/Nelson, May 1985; Molly White and Robert J. Cameron, *The Portage Early Educational Programme – A Practical Manual* (Revised version), Slough, NFER/Nelson, September 1987.

## CHAPTER 5

# The School Years

### Parents Talking

I find it very hard having my daughter home for five weeks' summer holiday. I think they should have some day centres open during the summer holidays.

When we went to hospital once and he had an operation it was the worst time of all as no one knew how to deal with a frightened boy. I was there, and they stayed clear. It was awful.

He attended a normal school at first, but I took him away from school after a few months. I taught him at home until he was accepted for the special school. Mainly I found the whole process of acceptance for school slow and hurtful – hurtful watching him at a normal school being bullied and upset. I felt it all unnecessary.

I found the workshops for parents run by staff at the school very helpful.

The school was not the right place for her. I had to fight with the local authorities for six months before she was placed in the correct one.

We didn't like him having to go away to school, but nothing else was available.

We managed fine during the holidays, although I feel it would be helpful for there to be more supervised recreational facilities during the summer holidays as there are for children who do not suffer from learning difficulties.

We were fairly happy with his school eventually, but we did wish that we could have been given a choice and not just told where he was to go.

We were not happy when he was in the ordinary school, because it was obvious that in the ordinary school our child was a target for teasing which made him very unhappy and an outcast.

From reports and comments made by the parents in the survey it is clear that in many ways the school years are, for the majority, by far the least stressful period of their experience. This even applies to the parents of the older and adult handicapped, although the 'education' their children were given was very limited by today's standards. Sadly there is an inverse correlation in that those most in need, namely the most severely handicapped, as for example the rubella-damaged deaf/blind, are the least likely to be properly catered for. This will be discussed further later in this chapter. There are many reasons why the situation is improved for the parents when schooldays start, but the basic one is that it marks the end of isolation; from then on much is made easier, for they have become part of a community whose main purpose is to help them achieve the things they wish for their children. A simple example of this is the greater help they get in obtaining dental care.

The passing of the Education Act of 1981 in many ways initiated a new chapter and a new outlook. Following on the recommendations of the Warnock Report it gives legal recognition to the parents' right to be consulted when major decisions regarding their handicapped children's education are being made. It also acknowledges the part that parents can and sometimes do play in their handicapped children's education. Until this 1981 Act replaced it, the Education Act of 1944 (although with several amendments and supplementary Acts) remained the legal basis of Special Education; and before going on to consider the Warnock Report and the Act of 1981 it is interesting to look at the way parents were regarded under the earlier Act and the role they were expected to play. It was the duty of the local education authority to have regard for parents' anxieties about their children for children aged two and above. The authorities also had to give written notice to the parents that it was being considered whether their child needed extra help. If the parents objected to the decision that their child did need a place in a special school then the authority had to proceed to certify that the child required it. If this was done and the parents still wished to oppose it, they had to appeal to the Minister of Education, who alone had the right either to cancel or to approve the certification. In other words, under this Act the parents' rights were very limited, consisting solely of:

- being able to request a medical examination, which could be refused if the education authority considered it to be unreasonable;
- being present at the medical examination; and
- the right of appeal to the minister against the authority's decision.

It is worth noting that, although the authority had to tell the parents the decision that had been made, no one was obliged to tell them of their right of appeal. The parents had a duty to produce their child for the medical examination and they could be forced to comply with the decision that had been made. It would not be a true picture of what actually happened, however, if the impression was left that the Act was applied with full vigour. Normally it was appreciated that it was far better in the interests of all, not least the child, if willing co-operation was secured. Parents were frequently kept well informed and consulted, but it was not their right; so they were not always consulted, and much resentment was often felt in consequence.

Many of the parents reacted to this by joining and forming the mutual aid societies, because it was soon appreciated that far more attention was paid to a body of opinion than to an individual's view. This led in turn to a growth of public interest. Among the professionals there was increasing interest in and research into the problems and possibly undeveloped potential of the handicapped. Public and professional interest so combined brought about the belief that the whole basis of providing Special Education needed to be reconsidered. This led in turn to the setting up of the Warnock Committee, which resulted in the Warnock Report.

## The Warnock Report

A Committee of Inquiry into the Education of Handicapped Children and Young People was first proposed in November 1973 with the following terms of reference, as stated by Margaret Thatcher, the then Secretary of State for Education:

> To review educational provision in England, Scotland and Wales for children and young people handicapped by disability of body or mind, taking account of the medical aspects of their needs, together with arrangements to prepare them for entering into employment, to consider the most effective use of resources for these purposes and to make recommendations.

This Committee was established in 1974 under the chairmanship of Mrs (now Lady) H. M. Warnock and first met in September of that year. Its report, entitled *Special Educational Needs*, was published in May 1978.[1] The report covered the whole age range from infancy to adulthood and emphasised three main areas as priorities for better provision. They were:

- The pre-school years.
- The post-school years.
- Teacher training.

One of the report's basic conclusions was that there is no point of separation between the handicapped and the non-handicapped, but a continuum. From this it follows that the assumption that at one particular point of the scale children need Special Schools is untenable. The Warnock Committee accepted that many more children, namely one in five rather than the previously accepted one in fifty, were in need of special help at some time during their school years. It also recognised that for educational purposes it was not appropriate to categorise children according to a medical diagnosis of handicap. The concept of *special educational needs* was proposed in its place. These needs should be determined by a multi-disciplinary and detailed analysis of the child's strengths and weaknesses and should take account of educational, psychological and medical factors. They should also take account of an assessment of the resources and deficiencies of his or her setting, thus emphasising the parental role, and also of the fact that Special Education should be defined in terms of what it consists of rather than where it takes place. Any child who for any reason had a learning difficulty which called for special educational provision was a child with special needs.

Importantly in the context of this book, the Warnock Report also stressed the role of the parents and the importance of establishing and maintaining co-operation with them in everything relating to their child's assessment as having any special needs.

The Government White Paper of August 1980 and the Education Act of 1981 which followed incorporated many of the recommendations of the Warnock Report.

**The Education Act of 1981**

This Act, which became operational in April 1983, repealed all provisions in previous Education Acts relating to Special Education and established a new framework for it in ordinary and in special schools. As postulated by Warnock, it accepted that 20 per cent, or one in five, of pupils of school age would have special needs at some time during their school life because of 'learning difficulty'. This term includes not only physical and mental disorder but also any kind of learning difficulty experienced by a child which is significantly greater than that of the majority of children of the same age.

Subject to four conditions the Act established the principle that all children determined by the local education authority as being in need of special educational provision should receive this provision in ordinary schools. The conditions were as follows:

1. Parents' views.
2. The ability of the school to meet the child's needs.
3. The provision of efficient education for other children in the school.
4. The efficient use of resources by the local education authority.

This part of the Act has been widely criticised as being too general and too flexible, in that it offers too much opportunity for those local education authorities that do not wish to redesign their educational provisions to offer reasons why they should not do so, since practically all inaction could be justified, if it was so desired, under one or other of these conditions. This topic merits wide discussion but it is outside the main purpose of this book and will not be pursued further here.

Among the other provisions of the 1981 Act are an amendment of the duties of the school governors and a restatement of the powers of local education authorities to provide home tuition, tuition in hospitals and teachers in adult training centres. It also extends the period of responsibility for children with special educational needs at both ends of the normal school age range, starting at age two and, if required, continuing to the age of nineteen for those pupils still at school. It states that the health authorities have a duty to inform both the parents and the education authority if, in their opinion, a child from birth to five years has, or is likely to have, special educational needs. This is a very useful and important change, since it ensures that help is available to the child and the parents at the earliest possible age. This has important consequences both for the child's future and for the parents' relief and ease of mind.

There are many other important provisions in this Act which cannot be discussed here since again they lie outside the main theme of this book. It is, however, relevant to consider its statements on the rights of parents. Some people have dubbed the Act 'The Parents' Charter', and there is some validity in this, for the Act does specify, as no other Act has done, what are the rights of the parents. Firstly, as regards the assessment by the education authority of children needing special educational provision, it states that:

1. The authority must notify the parents of the intention to assess.
2. Parents have the right to be given information about the procedure.
3. Parents have the right to make representations within twenty-one days.
4. Parents have the right to know whether the authority is to proceed with the assessment.
5. Parents have the right to be given information about a Statement of Special Educational Needs.
6. The local education authority is required to give parents the name of an officer from whom they can obtain any further information they may require.
7. Parents must be notified of their right to appeal to the Secretary of State, if the authority decides, after assessment, not to determine the special educational provision to be made for their child.
8. Parents must receive a draft Statement if the authority has decided that a Statement is necessary.

(These Statements are drafted after a full assessment of the child by all concerned, including the parents, has been made. They are a summary of the child's special needs and are required when an authority has decided *either* that extra resources in terms of staffing or equipment would be required to cater for those needs in an ordinary school, or that those needs can be most efficiently met in a special school.)

9. If the child is under the age of two the local education authority has the power to assess it, with the consent of the parents. If the parents ask for an assessment the L.E.A. is required to make it and can then under these

requirements make a Statement in whatever way they consider to be appropriate.

10. If a Statement has been made, the local education authority has the duty to make special educational provision accordingly. The parents, having received the draft Statement, then have the right (which they must be told about) to make any representations they wish, within a fifteen-day period. They also have the right to request an interview with either an officer of the authority or any person who gave advice as part of their child's assessment or some other person qualified to discuss the matter.
11. The formal Statement must be prepared by the authority in the manner prescribed by the Secretary of State, and a copy must be given to the parents, accompanied by notice of their right of appeal, plus the name of a person from whom they can get advice or information should they wish for it.
12. The parents have the right of appeal to a local appeal committee. This committee cannot overrule the authority if it disagrees with its proposals, but it can refer the case back to the authority for reappraisal in the light of its observations; and then the authority must reconsider but not necessarily alter its decision.
13. If, ultimately, the parents are still not satisfied, then they have the right to appeal to the Secretary of State, who alone has the power, as under the previous Act, to confirm, amend or negate the decision made by the authority.

The contrary situation may arise when the parents wish for an assessment and Statement to be made but the authority feels that the child's needs can be met without going through the formal procedure. In this case the authority must comply unless it feels the request is unreasonable. Here again if the parents' wishes are not met they have the right of appeal to the Secretary of State.

Comparing these statements of the parents' rights with those conferred by the 1944 Act, it is clear that much greater recognition is now legally given to the extent of the parents' involvement in decisions regarding their child. There are some doubts, though, as to how far these rights are being observed. A report published by the Spastics Society in May 1986 of a study carried out by the Centre for Studies in Integration (which is part of the Spastics Society) shows that these doubts have some justification.[2] Half of the sixty-five English and Welsh authorities surveyed did not fully inform the parents in a way that could be understood of the assessment process and the part they should play in it. Only 14 per cent told the parents that they must be treated as partners, and an even smaller percentage mentioned that the policy was to integrate children with special needs in ordinary schools wherever possible. It seems highly unlikely, if the parents are not made aware of this, that they are told of the options which should be available to them or given any opportunity to see and assess them for themselves. Frequently they seem to have the impression that there is no option, and realistically this is often the case; either the alternatives do not exist, or distance makes them unavailable. The survey makes other cogent criticisms. It seems that there is still a long way to go even though the legal position is quite clear.

### *Some Reservations Regarding the 1981 Act*

Important though the improvements brought about by the 1981 Act are, nevertheless some reservations have to be expressed. For example, although the consent of the parents has to be obtained before a child under the age of two can be assessed by the local education authority, this is not the case after that age. The obligation then is for the authority to notify parents of its intention to assess and to take note of any representations they may make. The decision as to whether to go ahead, however, rests with the authority. Similarly, if it is decided that a Statement should be made, then the authority decides on the provision to be made in accordance with the Statement. It will normally be the case (one hopes) that every effort will be made to obtain parental agreement, but if this does not prove to be possible then the decision rests with the authority and can be altered only if, as is rarely the case, the Secretary of State on appeal comes to a different decision.

The parents at times feel outnumbered by the professionals, and indeed this is the case. They are also most often far less practised in presenting their views, which hinders them when, for instance, they are invited to do this on the relevant form which is sent to them with the draft Statement. At every stage parents should be given the name of someone to refer to, but this is only fruitful if they take advantage of it. In turn this will depend to a large extent on the way their inquiries are received. Fundamental to all this is the underlying attitude of the authority and the professionals: whether they do honestly regard the parents as contributing partners or, as has frequently been the case, only as clients to be guided and advised. In some ways, although this is now against the present stated policy, the Act would seem to support the latter view. Closer inspection of its recommendations shows that, although it is stressed that the parents must be asked to give their views and to be kept informed at every stage, they do not have freedom of choice among what options may exist, nor do they take part in any actual decision-making.

It has to be remembered that there is no one model for the parents of handicapped children, for they come from every stratum of society and vary as do all other members of the community in their abilities, attitudes and experience. Some are able and articulate, others are not, but they all have a right to be heard. Ways have to be devised to communicate with them all and to help those who are inexperienced and inarticulate to overcome these problems.

**Parents as Partners**

There are two main areas in which parents can and should be involved as partners: (1) in intervention and (2) in assessment. At the present time there are many ways in which parents are accepted as partners in intervention techniques. Portage is a good example, and also the different ways in which parents are now involved in reading programmes. Other examples could be given. Less attention has been given to the value of parents as partners in assessment. This is odd, since they are the undisputed experts in the knowledge of their own children, the family and their environment. Moreover, they also have a particular knowledge of the school their child has attended, the way it has appeared to them and their child's reactions to it – all of which factors have relevance and importance. Their knowledge complements that of the school and the other professionals concerned; and when consultation does take place, both sides are often equally surprised by what they learn from each other!

Local authorities are aware of their obligation to communicate with parents, and normally the first line of communication when a school-age child is concerned is through the headteacher or teachers of the school which the child attends. If it is felt that the child should be assessed, then the usual practice is for the authority to send an official letter to the parents, which can and should include an explanation of the procedure which will follow and guidelines to assist the parents. A typical letter of this kind sent out by one authority also made the suggestion that the parents should, if they felt the need, seek advice and help from a voluntary organisation concerned with children with special needs. This seems to be a helpful idea, since many parents in such circumstances want reassurance and an opinion separate from that offered by the local authority.

Although these letters are helpful and fully informative, they are also of necessity official in form and could even be rather daunting in the amount of information they give. Personal help from a voluntary society as suggested is one way of coming to understand them; another is the use of a supplementary booklet which deals with the same information in a much less formal way. An excellent example of this is the booklet *What Now?* produced by the Surrey County Council Psychological Service.[3] This explains in simple terms the steps which will be followed and then goes on to quote and answer the questions most frequently asked by the parents – questions usually prefixed by 'What do I do . . .?' or 'What happens then . . .?' The booklet also includes a simple explanation of the terms frequently used to describe children's learning problems, and then goes on to suggest guidelines to help the parents set out the information they wish to give regarding their child and the points they wish to make. Other agencies have produced similar guidelines, which vary in minor ways, but they all give clear guidance as to what information is useful to give and how it can be described under the general headings on the official form. Any of those available would certainly be most helpful to parents who may be unsure both of what kind of information is required when their views are asked for and also how to set these views out.

**Consequences of the 1981 Act**

Although the Act became law in 1981 it did not become operative until 1983. In many ways it is therefore far too soon to discuss its consequences in all but the most general terms. A great deal of alarm was caused in some schools, which felt that the Act spelt their closure. This was particularly true, perhaps, of the schools for the Educationally Subnormal (Moderate) [ESN (M)]; for it was clear that with the wider definition of children with special needs many of the children attending them were similar to those who had remained in the ordinary schools but whose needs had frequently not been recognised or catered for.

This statement is borne out by the surveys carried out since the then Minister of Education in 1961 invited local education authorities to provide facilities for 'backward' pupils in ordinary schools (*Circular 11/61*).[4] By 1968, of the 12,807 pupils found to be requiring such provision, only 6,892 (54 per cent) were receiving it. This proportion was confirmed by later surveys. In a booklet published in 1982 W. K. Brennan goes even further when he states that only three out of every six slow learners in ordinary schools were in schools making any attempt to meet their special needs, and of those 'only one is likely to be in a school which is successfully meeting their special needs'.[5]

If, however, in consequence of the Act this situation is to be improved it is highly probable that most children from the ESN (M) range in particular will be considered to be suitably provided for in normal schools. In this particular case parents' wishes could and should play a decisive part. Some parents have indicated that they would welcome the transfer; others are more cautious, remaining as yet unconvinced of either the social or the educational advantages that it is argued would follow. Some feel that their children are much happier in the smaller special school, where they have much more chance of knowing and being known by everybody. Others too are anxious that the return to normal school would be more likely to bring a return of the teasing which their children suffered before they were transferred to the special school.

There is a certain amount of evidence that the parents whose children have moved from ordinary schools to special schools are the ones most likely to resist integration, while the parents of those children who have been in special schools from the beginning (mainly the most severely handicapped) are frequently the ones who are pressing hardest for it. Many reasons are put forward by them for wanting it, such as wanting the handicapped child to go to the same school as his or her brothers and sisters; but it may also be important that these parents have not had the experience of seeing how their child fares in a mainstream school.

In this context an interesting article, written by the mother of a brain-damaged girl was published in the Education section of the *Guardian* newspaper early in January 1987. The mother was a firm supporter of integration, and her daughter was admitted to a normal school when the time came for her to start. The headteacher and staff throughout were sympathetic, co-operative and supportive and had carefully prepared the other children. For the first two years it appeared to be a success. However, as the children grew older and bigger the differences in performance and behaviour maturation between the little girl and the other children became marked, and she became confused and unhappy in many ways. The parents therefore, purely in the interests of the child, made the decision to move her to a special school, where she is happy and successful. The mother is now fighting to stop this school from being closed. In the article she poses a fundamental and important question when she ponders whether in fact it was herself and her husband – the parents – who needed integration more than the child did.

Similar experiences have been reported about, for example, children with Down's syndrome who can often be contained happily in an infants school but cannot cope as they get older. It would be wrong to generalise from a few examples, but it is to be hoped that this question will be properly researched as the weight of evidence grows with the passing of time.

As is the case when a child is being assessed, it has been found that there is a great deal of variation in the practices of the local education authorities in the extent to which they are implementing the Act. Some actively make every effort to meet its implied requirements; others are doing relatively little to change their existing policies. A survey made in 1983 of local education authorities found that only one-third were prepared to alter their practices.[6] However, general agreement exists that, especially in the primary schools, intellectually able but physically handicapped children are the most easy to integrate and show the most success in all respects, both educationally and socially.

At present integration seems to be most common and most successful in infant and primary schools. There are obvious reasons for this, among them the larger size of the secondary schools, plus the growing complexity of the subjects taught and the need for pupils to go to different areas for different subjects. These factors all greatly increase the problems of organisation and of providing a wide range of suitable teaching techniques.

Of necessity these observations are based only on preliminary findings. There are many questions unanswered as yet which time alone will help to resolve. What is already clear is that in all circumstances certain criteria have to be met if any success is to be achieved. Some of these have already been discussed, namely:

- The school's ability to cater for the needs of all its pupils, the able as well as those with special needs.
- That the interests of either group are not adversely affected by the presence of the other.
- That resources can be used effectively.

Of equal importance are the attitudes of the staff and the parents. It is essential that the teaching staff are willing to accept 'special' children and are prepared to co-operate fully in their education. For this to become a reality, the teachers must be consulted and given all the relevant information they will need to accommodate the child successfully in their group. This is far from always being the case at present. It is not always the obvious problems that are the most relevant; even a simple thing like a child having poor bladder control can cause acute distress and embarrassment to all concerned if the teacher has not been told. They also need firm assurances that the necessary back-up and support services will be available.

The parents of the normal children in the school must be willing to accept the introduction of the handicapped children, and for this they, like the teachers, need to know what will be involved and be given assurances that the education of their children will not be adversely affected; while the parents of the handicapped need to have genuine choice and to have their wishes respected. Unless this willingness and consent is obtained from all concerned there is little hope, if any, that such educational integration will succeed.

**The Derbyshire Review**

In 1984 Derbyshire County Council sought the comments of parents, professionals and organisations involved in the multi-professional assessment of pupils with special need in Derbyshire.[7] Contributors were also invited to make further comments on the total return. This review is important not only because it gives a clear picture, scientifically gathered, of the views of the people concerned, but also because it was intended to form the basis for the county's development of the service.

A questionnaire was sent to a 10 per cent sample of those parents whose children had been given a multi-professional assessment. The children were placed subsequently in all the different forms of special education, which consisted of units, out-county schools, special schools, mainstream schools with welfare assistance, home tuition and those receiving extra teaching time. An unusually high proportion (76 per cent) of the questionnaires were returned. The questions asked were simple and factual, such as, 'How did you first learn that your child may have special educational needs?', 'Were you able to express your views on the assessment procedure?' and 'How can the service be improved?'

Some interesting comments were made in reply to this last question, for example:

> More contact with the parents.
>
> Less paperwork, less formality.
>
> Money! Obviously more special teachers are needed.
>
> Educational psychologists should spend more time and get to know a child. It takes a long time to get the confidence of any child.

The question, 'What in your opinion could be changed for the better?' evoked a similar reply to the last: 'The educational psychologist needs to get to know the children better. I wanted more involvement with my child's education to help him at home.'

This comment has validity and could well be echoed by most educational psychologists; for even though in many areas more psychologists are being employed, in most areas their case-load is still very heavy. In addition, the extra paperwork that implementing the 1981 Act involves takes up a great deal of the time which could otherwise have been given to getting to know the child. Catch-22.

Other changes which the parents felt could be helpful are very revealing, for example: 'More regard to parents' views. No amount of professional training can give the feeling of despair a parent experiences before the problem is identified' – a comment which in different ways comes up in every chapter of this book. Several parents wanted the procedures to be speeded up, an interesting pointer to the degree of tension and anxiety they were feeling. One other revealing comment was that there 'should be more discussions about home background and any pressure parents may be under'.

When asked to 'rate the service given to yourself and your child',

58 per cent rated it as 'very good';
24 per cent rated it as 'good';
17 per cent rated it as 'average';
0 per cent rated it as 'poor';

and one parent rated it as only 'very poor' but qualified this by adding, 'But only at the beginning.' The authority justifiably concludes: 'Most parents are satisfied with the service provided.'

The considerations which the survey revealed as appearing to be of most importance to the parents were:

1. The opportunity to talk to others with knowledge of the difficulties being experienced by the child and themselves.
2. Reassurance as to the nature of the difficulty, proposal for action and subsequent provision to meet special needs.
3. Being consulted and feeling that they, as parents, had an active role to play.
4. The feeling that something was being done.

A minority of the parents expressed some dissatisfaction about a few parts of the service, one of which is undoubtedly shared by everybody with any experience or knowledge of this field, and that is a concern over the level of the resources allotted to pupils with special educational needs. Other criticisms seemed to stem from the parents' own emotions and unresolved feelings of guilt and a lack of acceptance of the child's disabilities. Sadly these feelings of self-blame are common to a greater or lesser degree to all parents of handicapped children and are extremely difficult to resolve. Intellectually it is possible to help the parents to see that they are unjustified, but there always appears to be a deep-seated core of emotion which cannot be eliminated. It is possibly an attempt to deal with this that led to some of the parents expressing the feeling that they should be allowed or expected to do more; likewise their frustrations over apparent delays in responding to the child's (and their) needs, and also their feeling of not being able to convince the professionals of their real concerns regarding their child. This latter point has been expressed (at times forcibly) by other parents in other parts of the country. There may well be truth in it, since it is an established fact that people tend to see what they are looking for. It clearly highlights the importance of consultation and genuine communication, not merely 'lip-service'. Finally, and it should be stressed that this is a minority feeling; some parents did feel that the interviews were too hurried, the documentation was too formal and both interview and documentation were 'insensitive'.

The questionnaire was also sent to the psychologists, who had a different section to complete. In this section the psychologists considered many of the administrative details. A number of them went on to make the point that

> The provision of psychological time to meet the requirements of the 1981 Act had been seriously underestimated. . . . Conflicting demands were being placed on psychologists between doing statutory work on the one hand, and preventative school-based work on the other. . . . Educational psychologists need more time.

With regard to parental involvement, two general points were made. The first supports the view already discussed in this chapter that there is a need for guidelines to assist parents in making their reports. The second point 'urged that schools be encouraged to take a more structured approach to their work with parents, particularly prior to the initiation of the multi-professional assessment'.

This is interesting, because there are obvious advantages in a structured approach in general. But in view of the comments made by some of the parents it would appear to be more fruitful to keep the approaches on a friendly and informal basis within an overall basic structure.

The third section of the review, which sets out the views and comments of the headteachers and staffs of special schools and units, contains much of interest. For example, the observation was made that there was a 'danger in professionals becoming report-orientated and not child-orientated'. The view is also supported that 'there was clear shortage of educational psychologist time'. The greater role played by the parents in the multi-professional procedures was welcomed by the schools, but whereas the parents reported frustration over delay, the heads and schools felt 'that the exercise of the parental right to further discussion, consultation and dialogue prolonged the time taken in meeting a child's special educational needs'. One implication that could be drawn from this comment would be that the schools felt that their recommendations must be correct; if this were not the case there is surely no room for questioning the time taken to reach the correct solution. Taking this a little further, it indicates that the old view of parents as 'clients' rather than 'partners' still holds to some extent.

This impression comes over more strongly in a later section of the review, which deals with the comments made by teacher associations and voluntary groups: 'Several contributors expressed concern that parental wishes were often counter to the child's best interest.' And again the comment is made that 'the amount of extra parental involvement . . . slows up the progress of the child'. No proof is given to support this statement. As did the head-teachers of the special schools, the mainstream primary and secondary school heads 'generally welcomed the greater involvement of the parents'; 'Parents appreciate that they are consulted throughout. This makes them realise more that our major concern, like theirs, is the progress of the child.'

Section six of the review reports on the remarks made by the advisory services and says, regarding parental involvement, that 'the increasing parental demand for information on the new arrangements' is obvious. Secondly, it reports: 'A request was made for in-service training in schools on the policy of "parents as partners" ' – an interesting request in view of the opinions from the schools quoted above.

Finally, three further points regarding the parents were made by the area health authorities and the social services representatives. Firstly, there was a general feeling that parents would benefit from knowing more of 'what the procedures are all about'. Secondly, parents were reported as sometimes feeling very intimidated by the variety and number of professionals involved in the assessment of their child. And thirdly, a point which follows on, 'the obvious anxieties of parents and the extent to which the bureaucratic formalities of the Act exacerbate these anxieties' were remarked on.

Many other related topics are covered by this very comprehensive review. The account here has been focused on those parts of it which relate to the parents and their involvement. It is clear from the review's findings, which it should be stressed are to be the basis for development, that the greater part to be played by the parents under the Act has been welcomed, and also that the parents in return are very appreciative of this. Obviously at this early stage much can be improved, but it is very hopeful that, in Derbyshire at least, the improvements when they come will be firmly based on the practical and combined experiences of all those involved, including the parents.

It is already apparent that two major difficulties will have to be resolved. Firstly, all the professionals independently report in their separate comments on the amount of time involved in fulfilling the requirements of the Act and their anxieties as to how that time can be spent without detriment to their other obligations. Secondly, there is the total impossibility of providing all that is felt to be necessary from, as the Act requires, 'within their existing resources'. Apart from this, there is little doubt that most if not all the other problems can be overcome with co-operation and continuing goodwill. Ultimately, however, the question will have to be faced as to whether the present policy can be proved to be the best possible for the children and their parents.

## Special Problems

In general there is little doubt that since the 1944 Act there has been a vast improvement in the education provided for children with special needs, and also a great increase in the concern and respect shown to their parents. It is too soon as yet to evaluate the changes which it is hoped will be brought about by the implementation of the Education Act of 1981. In many areas the changes have not even started. However, whatever the outcome, research and evaluation will undoubtedly continue for as long as professional and public interest is active. Dangers will arise if the passing of the Act is assumed to mean that its recommendations thereby become effective.

But, even supposing the maximum is achieved with time and, most importantly, an increase in resources, there will still be a relatively small body of children for whom the provision made is either non-existent or unsatisfactory. These are the children with the greatest needs: the most severely handicapped. Among these are the children with multiple handicaps of various kinds, and in particular those children who without very skilled help either do not or cannot communicate because of their handicaps: children such as the deaf/blind, the psychotic and the autistic. It is quite clear from the Education Act that special schools will continue to exist for those whose needs are judged to require more than any ordinary school could be expected to provide. This is the case with some of the children previously designated ESN (S), for example, and there are enough of such children to ensure that a school can be provided for them within their own area. This is not the case with the deaf/blind and with the autistic and psychotic children. Their parents are frequently faced with the dilemma of either accepting provision which they do not feel is appropriate, or agreeing to their child travelling long distances daily to a more suitable school, or accepting a boarding placement for them. There are valid objections made by parents to all of these possibilities.

The situation is further complicated by the fact that it is extremely difficult because of their handicaps to make a correct assessment both of the needs and of the potential of these children. Not only have they little or no ability to communicate, but because of their condition they have also been deprived of many of the learning experiences a child normally has from birth. It is therefore very easy to assume from their level of performance that they are also mentally handicapped, and since a school for very retarded children is available to think that they are correctly placed there. This situation is one in which the expertise of parents should be regarded as invaluable, for they have the intimate knowledge of their child which no one else can hope to have. It is not the experience of many of the parents that this is either accepted or appreciated. The following were typical comments:

> I would have liked people to recognise my child's potential and listen to me, and I deeply resented having my child referred to as a case study.
>
> (Mother of an autistic child)

> The one thing that stands out about the whole experience is that you have to fight for everything, fight to find out the truth about your child and what is wrong, fight for benefits and allowances that should be yours by right, fight to get the school that is right for your child, fight to gain acceptance of your child. If only it was a bit less time-consuming on that side of things, the extra time your child demands wouldn't seem so bad.
>
> (Mother of a multiply handicapped child)

The mother of a deaf/blind child made a similar comment when she wrote:

> The school my child was sent to was not the correct place for her. I had to fight with the local authority before she was placed in the correct one. There was no understanding between me, the mother, and the local authority, if only we could have sat down together and discussed my daughter's future.

This, of course, should now be the accepted pattern, but whether or not it happens seems to vary considerably and to depend on the attitudes of the people involved. More than one parent remarked that 'The service you get is as good as the people who are working it.' A truism perhaps, but none the less valid.

If the correct school is available but at such a distance that the child has to make a long journey daily to get to it, the parents feel very cut off from the school and are anxious about many things, including the possible dangers inherent in the daily journey. Transport is usually provided by the authority either in hired cars or in minibuses. Invaluable though this facility is, it means that the day is even further lengthened for the child, because each vehicle has to be used to capacity to make the service as economical as possible, which means a roundabout trip. Other anxieties felt arise from the lack of close contact and the possible resulting difficulties in communication. The schools normally try to compensate with the use of 'home diaries' and similar devices, but these are frequently lost or not filled in by one side or the other, and even if they are perfectly kept they are a poor substitute for person-to-person contact. Another worry that arises as the child gets older is that his or her opportunities for making social and other contacts and relationships in his or her own area are considerably reduced.

These are some of the powerful arguments that were used when the decision was made that as many children with special needs as possible should attend the normal local school, but these are the children for whom the normal school cannot provide. At present there does not seem to be any answer suggested other than the impossible one of the affected parents moving to get near the special school. Some parents have certainly done this, but it is a high price to pay and it is not always either practical or possible.

Many of the same problems arise if a boarding placement is all that is available. One parent summed it up in this way:

> We had an impossible choice to make. We knew that the local school could not meet her needs properly, but how could we let her go to a boarding school? We had been working hard all her life to build up and establish a relationship with her and are just beginning to feel we are succeeding. We just can't risk losing this by letting her go.

The acute but not unique dilemma experienced by other parents is described by Margaret Brock as follows:

> He had been for eighteen months in a school where he was found to be ineducable, and ascertained mentally handicapped, and a year later found to have too high an IQ for the placement he then had, he was too blind for a deaf school and too deaf for a blind school. We had now come to the worst impasse of all by the hardest possible route, that of obeying every scrap of advice and of accepting every bit of help from all quarters.[8]

It is true that this particular boy is now grown up, but the same sort of situation can and does still happen. In all such cases a compromise solution has to be accepted, and the parents are almost invariably left with the perhaps unexpressed feeling that the outcome for their child would have been better if this had not been the case.

Since the passing of the 1981 Act it should have been possible to improve this situation, but one of the facts that has prevented this is that there are very few teachers available in the whole of the country who have the necessary training and professional expertise to meet these children's needs. This is particularly true of the deaf/blind, and the situation is unlikely to improve since there is as yet no approved training course available for those who would wish to undertake it. The few who are so trained have had to go abroad for the training. The only alternative available is to take separately the authorised diplomas available for the teachers of the deaf and the teachers of the blind.

In addition, because of falling school rolls, schools and units for the deaf and blind are being closed on a local basis with no overall planning. In consequence some local areas have more provision than they need, others none at all. In the summer of 1982 there were thirteen deaf/blind units; by 1984 three had closed, two more were closed in November 1985, another one was under threat of immediate closure and four had been changed to units for multiply handicapped deaf children. This meant that there were then in the whole country only three units specifically providing for the deaf/blind. At the same time, careful research had identified no less than seventy deaf/ blind children, and a survey had shown that large numbers were in schools for children with severe learning difficulties.

It is not surprising that SENSE (the National Deaf/Blind and Rubella Association) has set up a working party for 'Considering Education for Deaf/Blind Children.' In the words of Paul Ennals, SENSE's head of welfare services, 'It has been a long-running saga, awaiting something definite from the Department of Education and Science.'[9] Hopes were raised when it was arranged for a delegation to meet the then minister, Sir Keith Joseph. But there is still 'nothing concrete on the table'. There is now a new minister. Meanwhile these children continue to be neglected. Until they and others in similar case are better provided for, there is no room for any complacency about the care we provide for our children with 'special needs'.

## Notes

1. Warnock Report, *Special Educational Needs*, Report of the Committee of Inquiry into the Education of Handicapped Children and Young People, London, HMSO, 1978.
2. Spastics Society Centre for Studies in Integration, *Caught in the Act: A Survey and Handbook*, London, Spastics Society, May 1986.
3. Schools Psychological Service, *What Now? Questions and Answers for Parents*, Surrey County Council, 1985.
4. *Circular 11/61*, Ministry of Education, 1961.
5. W. K. Brennan, *The Search for Quality: Special Education in Mainstream Schools*, Stratford-on-Avon, National Council for Special Education, 1982, p. 10.
6. Advisory Centre for Education, 'Slow progress in integration', *Where*, no. 187, pp. 15–16.
7. Julian Kramer, 'The 1981 Education Act in Derbyshire', *Special Education*, vol. 12, no. 3, 1985, pp. 96–101; also unpublished full report, '1981 Education Act: Special Educational Needs. Review of Procedures', 1984.
8. Margaret Brock, *Christopher: A Silent Life*, London, Bedford Square Press, 1975 and 1984, pp. 55–6.
9. Paul Ennals, head of welfare services, SENSE, Private letter.

CHAPTER 6

# And After School – What?

## Parents Talking

We think about what will happen to our daughter – but we try to take one day at a time.

I found this very difficult to answer when faced with questions I had not looked into so deeply and think it best not to. Just accept and make the best, and try to improve what you have. Only look forward – never back.

Although our daughter is still very young, one of my greatest concerns has always been what will happen to her when I die or am unable to look after her. I know there is no happy answer, and with the economy being as it is facilities and job prospects are not likely to improve. I cannot bear to think about it.

In an ideal world somebody would take on responsibility for him and look after him. I don't believe he should be in an institution even when I die.

We all love our 'special child' very much. But he should, and we have to let him, live away and become independent of us, his family, as we cannot always be there. We do not, however, want to sentence him to an institutional life where he will be forgotten.

Fears for the future always lurk in the back of my mind and the constant feeling of what will happen when loving parents aren't around to care for their child.

I hate to think that she will need to go into a hospital with no individuality of her own. She has plenty going for her if it can be exploited.

There was never any discussion or information from our local social services about what will happen when he reaches school-leaving age. In fact, he has never had a social worker visit him. We are in the process of moving to Cumbria where the Social Services Department seems to be much more helpful.

> As with everything else, the question of money is paramount, and the majority of local authorities are very reluctant to spend it on the provision of facilities for the handicapped. Therefore it is very often left to the parents with the help of a few voluntary organisations to look after the handicapped child.
>
> There should be a double-check system to make sure a handicapped child is allotted to a social worker. In our case we were unaware we had a social worker until he was nearly sixteen, when one popped up to ask what we were doing about further education.
>
> I would like to know that, when I die or become unable to take care of him, he will have a safe and secure place to live and someone to look after him. I would like to be certain that any money I leave will be used for him and, hopefully, to take advantage of any new treatments which may become available.
>
> Most of the people in power seem to think that the containment of the handicapped child is sufficient, and this is very often in some sort of institution.

It is no exaggeration to say that the one question which is always in the mind of the parents of a handicapped child is, 'What will happen to our child when we are no longer able to care for him/her?' Until the time comes for the child to leave school they have dealt with it in many ways. Some, for example, do all they possibly can to make whatever financial provision they can afford; some hope that other members of the family will take over; while others, as one mother put it, 'really don't know the answer to the question. It is a worry that I can only cope with by not really facing up to it.' Many parents report that in all the early years they have found that the only way to survive is 'to take one day at a time'. There are so many things to do and so many immediate difficulties and problems to be dealt with, they just do not have either the mental or the physical energy to look too far ahead. So 'you either push it to the back of your mind, or worry at it like a dog with a bone, depending on your mood'. However, as the time for school-leaving approaches, the question of 'What comes next?' has to be faced.

For some the immediate answer is to postpone the decision for as long as possible by keeping their child in school until the maximum age of nineteen is reached. Then, if possible, they extend the period even further by using whatever facilities are available for further education and training. Further education is undoubtedly to the child's advantage (although, strictly speaking, it is now a young adult being considered); for it is nowadays accepted by all that abilities and capacities continue to develop and do not, as was previously believed, reach their full capacity in late adolescence. This age can also be an important period for personal development. The Warnock Report made the further point that, if opportunities were not available for continuing appropriate education, 'all the earlier efforts . . . may come to nothing'.[1]

Until very recently however, the scope of further education available was very limited, being mainly thought of as a continuance of developing literacy skills. It is now becoming appreciated that education should have a much wider meaning, particularly in relationship to the development of social skills, motivation and vocational interests. As with nearly everything else, these things may be appreciated but are far from adequately supplied. Suitable further education is available only for the fortunate few, and these are very often the ones whose parents have learnt how to 'fight'.

This word is one of the most frequently used:

> We had to fight . . . After the familiar fight . . .
>
> All you want is available if you know how to look for it – and are prepared to fight for it and at times even be prepared to move into another area to get the appropriate help.

One mother described her experiences in this way:

> I had to fight: write letters to national newspapers – local newspapers – 'sit in' outside the Director of Education's office – have spells of 'hysteria', etc. I wanted someone in power to speak up for me and not try to make me out to be just an anxious mother.

Once again it seems that the more handicapped the child, the greater the battle. For, as the mother of a multiply handicapped child reported: 'It is very difficult to get services or provision because of the multiple handicap; no one wants to accept responsibility.'

Looking again at the question, 'And after school – what?' it can be subdivided into three parts: 'What can my child do?', 'Where can he/she live?' and 'What will happen to him/her when I am no longer alive or can no longer cope?' Although the last of these is the one that parents find hardest to face, they are all matters of great anxiety. This is perhaps particularly true in the present time of financial stringency and high unemployment; but difficult though they are for parents to face, it is important to look at what is available.

**Further Education**

If parents choose further education as the immediate answer, the option of further education at school is open to all of their children up to the age of nineteen. This was clearly stated in the Act of 1944 and reaffirmed in the Act of 1981. The Warnock Report both recommended and emphasised the importance of continuing education 'for those young people with disabilities or significant difficulties who had reached or passed school-leaving age, but who were still progressing towards understanding and independence'.[2] It also made the provision of further education for young people over the age of sixteen with special educational needs one of its areas of main priority. The report stressed the importance of a reassessment of individual needs in the last years of school life and felt that the reassessment should be followed by a full discussion of the possibilities available involving all the professionals concerned, as well as the parents and, whenever possible, the pupils themselves.

Once again, some local authorities are putting this recommendation into effect, while others are not yet doing so. There is also a wide variety to be found in the options available. These seem to depend partly on the type of special needs and the ability of the pupil, partly on what is available, but mainly on the willingness of the local authority to provide them. So much concern was felt about this that a public campaign was initiated in 1983 by a group of organisations concerned with the needs of the handicapped and supported by the teachers' unions to insist that local authorities should carry out their legal obligations in this respect and make proper and adequate provision.

Several important surveys highlighted the need for this – for example, one carried out by the National Union of Teachers in 1983 to investigate local education authorities' provision for 16–19-year-olds with special educational needs.[3] This showed that of the fifty-two authorities that replied to the survey, only 17 per cent guaranteed a place either at college or in school to every young person wishing to continue their education. A further 10 per cent stated that they did not guarantee a place, while the remaining 73 per cent attached various conditions to their response to requests for places. This and other surveys produced irrefutable evidence that success in getting further education did not depend upon need, or even on what was available; the most important factor was simply where the parents happened to live. The recommendations made in the Warnock Report are, therefore, still a long way from being fulfilled. A different survey carried out in 1982 by the National Bureau for Handicapped Students revealed that one in three colleges of further education felt unable to provide for some physically handicapped students, and more than one in three felt unable to provide for the visually impaired and hearing handicapped.[4]

There is a further problem revealed in these surveys, ironically one which may have increased because of integration, and that is that far fewer handicapped people in the integrated schools have contact with the Careers Service than do the non-handicapped. This is not the case in special schools, where it is now common to find that planning and discussions do take place in the last two years of schooling.

Both new research and investigations of research being carried out are conducted by the Further Education Curriculum Review and Development Unit. This is an advisory, intelligence and development body for further education which was established in 1977 by the then Secretary of State for Education and Science. The National Foundation for Educational Research (NFER) has been commissioned by this body to carry out the actual investigations, and the Unit has produced two excellent and informative reports: *Students with Special Needs in Further Education*[5] and *Stretching the System*.[6] Both reports reveal that taken as a whole the situation is far from satisfactory, but they also discuss the implications of their findings and the issues that will need to be considered. With the benefit of such information there is hope that the future will bring about improvements, and importantly that these improvements will be based on a co-ordinated and cohesive approach.

Nevertheless, at present the main problem is that so few options are available, especially for children of limited intelligence and those who are multiply handicapped. These children have as much right as any other member of the community to have appropriate provision made for them. It is totally unacceptable that a parent should be made to feel that 'Most of the people in power seem to think that the containment of the handicapped child is sufficient, and this is very often in some sort of institution.'

## Other Options For Training And Employment

A very useful and interesting guide setting out the options for the school-leaver with special needs, and giving comprehensive advice on every aspect of after-school life, was produced under the auspices of the International Year of the Child Trust (IYC Trust) and published in 1985 by the National Children's Bureau.[7] The Trust was wound up in January 1983 but provided the necessary funds for the guide to be completed and published. This is an excellent production, full of practical guidance, and it should certainly be made available by the authorities to all such school-leavers and their parents.

However, excellent though this guide is, it does in a way highlight the problems of the more disabled, since so many of the facilities listed are beyond their reach. For them the options are very few. Some, as has been discussed, may appropriately stay on at school; others may stay not because it is appropriate but because nothing else is available. Although parents may to some extent be relieved that this is possible, they are also concerned, feeling correctly that although the child remains happy he or she should not still be in the environment which they first entered at the age of two or three. Parents often fear that this can prevent or delay maturation and social development. Yet they also cannot feel it appropriate that their child should leave school and remain aimlessly at home until a place becomes available in the only other option open to them, the Adult Training Centre or Social Education Centre. These will be discussed later in this chapter. There is another possibility for a few, and that is the provision made by some of the voluntary societies.

### *Provisions Made by Voluntary Societies*

Many of the voluntary societies do make some provision for children suffering from the particular handicap the society deals with, among them the National Society for Autistic Children and the Spastics Society. A good example of this sort of provision is the Manor House in Market Deeping, which was opened in 1980 by SENSE (the National Deaf/Blind and Rubella Association). It is the first rehabilitation and training centre in the country to care for the special needs of deaf/blind adolescents and young adults. It provides assessment, care and specialist training in such areas as communication, social skills and leisure activities, plus vocational training when appropriate in crafts, self-care, gardening and so on. One of the centre's main features is its appreciation of the need to form strong links with the local community – a necessary part of preparing these young people for more independent living. However, the Manor House can provide for only seventeen youngsters at a time, and they are admitted with no time limits. Inevitably in these circumstances to gain admission it has to be demonstrated that the youngster has the potential ability to benefit from the course provided. Those who gain admission are indeed fortunate – but what of the others?

It would seem yet again that the community as a whole is failing to develop for its handicapped members the facilities which have been proved to be helpful. In one way or another all of these young people will at some stage have to have provision made for them. It is incomprehensible why practical and proved facilities, such as the Manor House, funded and set up in the first place by voluntary organisations, are not developed and used as models for the provision which society must ultimately make. This is especially true since in many instances their cost compares very favourably with, for example, that of running a large hospital.

### *The Youth Training Scheme*

In considering this and the options which follow, it should be stated that they are all welcomed by the parents and gladly used if they are offered. Many of them are not options for the less able, however. The Youth Training Scheme (YTS) is run by the Manpower Services Commission but sponsored by several agencies including industrial and private employers. It is designed to help all young people to develop work skills, and disabled young people are eligible to join the scheme up to the age of twenty-one. There is also provision for them to stay longer on the scheme than the non-disabled if this is deemed to be helpful. A weekly allowance is paid to all those on the scheme. The parents of those accepted for YTS do feel positive towards it, because it not only increases the skills of their children but also provides them with a range of social experiences.

### *Employment Rehabilitation Centres*

When it is available this is an excellent scheme for more able youngsters. The centres offer courses which usually last for three months and are designed to give special work preparation to people with special needs, who, as in the YTS, are paid while they attend them. These schemes are very practically designed, teaching how to apply for a job, cope with an interview and so on. They also provide opportunities for the trainees to visit places of possible kinds of work and also to try them – an invaluable experience when it comes to making a decision.

### *Training Opportunities Scheme*

This scheme is designed for the possibly under-achieving but able young person. It is not run exclusively for people with special needs but is intended to supplement the qualifications of young people aged nineteen or over who have been out of work for at least two years. There are courses to coach those who are poor in reading and maths, plus a wide range of vocational training. People accepted for them receive a weekly personal allowance plus a needs allowance and travel expenses.

### *Registering as Disabled*

The above training schemes are all intended to give extra help and training to those young people with special needs who may ultimately find open employment. These young people and their parents will also have to decide whether or not they wish to be registered as disabled. There are practical advantages to be gained by those who choose to do so either on the local authority register or on the Disabled Persons' Register, both of which are voluntary. The first enables those registering to get help from the Social Services Department; the second is maintained under the Disabled Persons' (Employment) Act and is a register of disabled people who can work and wish to do so. It offers to those on its lists help with fares to and from work, special aids and equipment at work, sheltered employment and also access to those jobs which are reserved for disabled people. This is no mean advantage in the present climate of employment, since every employer of twenty or more people has legally to employ a percentage of registered disabled.

### *Sheltered Employment and Sheltered Workshops*

These sheltered forms of employment cater for those who even after further training cannot work in open employment and are registered disabled. They provide employment mainly for those with either physical, sensory or moderate learning disabilities. Some are run by local authorities, others by voluntary agencies or Remploy, a charity which is sponsored by local authorities. In order to obtain sheltered employment, it must first be decided that a particular workshop and job is suitable for the disabled person. This is usually established by a trial period, and the employee must be able to work regular hours. Those working in these workshops are paid the normal wages for the type of work they are doing. Allied to these sheltered workshops are the sheltered industrial groups, which consist of small groups of disabled people who work under supervision in an ordinary factory or workplace.

*Adult Training Centres*

All of these facilities are excellent and invaluable for those who can take advantage of them, but they cannot cater for the most severely mentally or physically disabled. For them the Adult Training Centre, or as they are now frequently called the Social Education Centre, remains the key resource. Many improvements have been, and are being, made in these centres, but they are on the whole limited by both insufficient resources and too large numbers. Parents are not unappreciative of what they have to offer but, understandably, wish that more could be done. Many of them come to feel that much that was gained by their children during the school years is lost when that period is over.

One of the several factors that cause some concern was expressed by one mother as follows: 'The other thing that bothers me is that when the children go to work centres then I wish that there could be a youth section for the ones that come from the schools so that they don't have to go with the older ones straight away.'

There is great variation in the way that the move from school to centre takes place, and it seems to depend on the philosophy of, and even the relationships that exist between, the head of the centre and the headteachers of the schools. Some centres offer a pattern of visits in the last school year; this is excellent, because in this way the young people get prepared for the move and know where they are going and what they will do when they get there. Some unfortunately do not, and it is not unknown for there to be no contact, even when the school and the centre share the same geographical site. However, this seems to be the exception rather than the rule.

In 1977 the National Development Group for the Mentally Handicapped published a pamphlet on *Helping Mentally Handicapped School-Leavers*.[8] In discussing the role of the Adult Training Centre, this document stressed the desirability of these centres assuming a broader educational role and linking effectively to further education arrangements as they may exist in the particular area. The word 'may' is particularly interesting in this context! Mary Warnock, in her 1978 brief guide, *Meeting Special Educational Needs*, makes the same point:

> All adult training centres and day centres should have a strong educational element. . . . If education is not provided and taken seriously and if highly professional teaching is not available a valuable period in the life of these young people will be wasted. Such education may make the crucial difference for them between a life of total dependence and one of reasonable freedom and purpose.[9]

The fact that these recommendations have rarely been fully implemented is not the fault of the centres, many of which do as much as is possible with their limited resources. Parents are concerned about the lack of stimulation and education provided, but, as they say repeatedly, 'We were not offered any choice.' It is not a good situation when after years of improving education all that is available at the age of nineteen is part-time attendance at a day centre, or a place in an overcrowded and underfunded Social Education Centre when a vacancy occurs, or a residential placement of one kind or another. It is no wonder that the common feeling is that more help and facilities should be available for the less able and that 'all the improvements made in recent years are geared to the benefit of the more able'.

## Where Shall They Live?

### *Living at Home*

Most parents, no matter how much they love their children, look forward to the time when they will leave home and establish their own homes and independence. However, parents of a child who is handicapped cannot assume that this will happen, and for many of them this is a worry that gets progressively worse as they and their child get older.

At present all the emphasis of society is on the value of living in the community, which for the recent school-leaver mainly means continuing to live at home. Some parents seem to accept this quite willingly, especially if they are able to get 'breaks' through the use of the respite or other services described earlier. Their main anxiety comes at the time when through changing circumstances or for other reasons they have to start considering what will happen to their children when they can no longer cope. When one considers what is involved in taking on the full-time, long-term care of a handicapped person one can only marvel that some parents manage for as long as they do. It is a perpetual strain both mentally and physically: mentally, because the care-giver's own life is inevitably affected both because of what has to be done for the handicapped and also because of the reduction in stimulus and social contacts in their own life it entails. Earlier in this book this was reported upon by parents caring for young handicapped children; but as the child gets older, far from improving, this becomes worse.

Every family responds in its own way. In some cases both parents are as involved as far as they are able to be, but someone usually has to go to work, and so the burden on one parent (most commonly the mother) is harder. In other cases where there are siblings they also are affected in one way or another. Here there appears to be a complete split – with a proportion of parents completely assuming that brothers and sisters will be involved, and the others determined that they should not be, except as people who will continue to take an interest in their 'special' brother or sister.

The following were typical comments:

> We do feel that his brother should not be given the burden, although we also hope and pray he would still love and keep in close contact with him.

> Whereas we have no wish to place the responsibility of his care on relations, as it is a great responsibility, we would hope that they will ensure that he is suitably placed in a setting which will meet his needs.

In some ways this says it all: 'suitably placed in a setting which will meet his needs'. It should not really be impossible for a relatively rich and sophisticated society such as ours to provide this. These same parents went on to say: '. . . Not forgetting our eldest daughter and her needs as well, as an individual; ensuring that she is not placed in a position of having to worry about her brother when she has her own life to lead.'

'As long as we can cope with him, he stays with us.' These simple words do not in any way reveal what is entailed, particularly for those caring for the severely handicapped: curtailment of social life and the need to go on year after year giving an increasingly older, and sometimes less manageable, adult all the bodily and physically demanding (often unpleasant) care that has to be given to a baby. At the same time, the carers are ageing and possibly developing physical problems of their own.

Even with full support services (and they are not always available) this is an onerous task. Nevertheless, there are a certain number of parents who state that brothers, sisters or other relatives will take on the care of the handicapped member of the family. If they willingly and voluntarily choose to do so then that is their right, and no comment can or should be made. It is perhaps not unfair to say that this choice would not be so frequently made, nor would some parents continue so long in caring, if they were happier about the alternatives available. What these alternatives are will now be considered, starting with those for the physically handicapped.

### *Council Housing and Housing Associations*

Some handicapped people, particularly those with a physical problem, are willing and able to live in a home of their own. Some local authorities cater for this by providing special housing of three kinds for physically handicapped people, the only problem with this being that it is in very short supply. Some housing associations exist which make similar provision.

The three kinds of housing provided are:

1. For those who use a wheelchair but are not confined to it.
2. For those who are dependent on a wheelchair for all their mobility; the accommodation is designed on one level and in such a way that access can be gained to all parts of it freely, using the wheelchair.

3. Sheltered housing, where groups of flats have a warden to provide whatever assistance is required.

One of these possibilities is obviously the best provision for those who are able enough to use it and lucky enough to be offered it. The rest must seek out and use whatever they find available.

*Hostels and Residential Homes*

For those who are not fully able to cope with independent living but either wish to live away from home or may have to because of their place of work or because they are attending a college or training scheme, there are some forms of accommodation available which also provide support, such as staffed group houses. These are run either by local authorities or by such organisations as the social work charities. Although the degree of freedom for the individual and the accommodation provided vary considerably, they do offer secure housing. However, it is also a more controlled way of life, since rules and regulations are inevitable in this type of provision.

*Housing for Mentally Handicapped People*

*Group homes (staffed or unstaffed)*
Group homes are run either by Social Services Departments or by voluntary agencies. They are, in fact, ordinary houses in the neighbourhood where small numbers of mentally handicapped people can live as in a family. Some have residential staff, others do not, although they are in the general care and under the supervision of social workers. This is intended to be a growing service, but it would be wrong to give the impression that it is generally available. It is also a cause of anxiety and concern to some people who feel that the policy is being started with too little preparation being provided for the intended residents and with too few supporting services being available. This is usually because of inadequate resources. This problem is exacerbated by the fact that people moved out of hospitals cease to be the financial responsibility of the health services and become the responsibility of the local authorities, and negotiating the financial transfer arrangements can cause considerable delays.

Another cause of anxiety, genuinely felt by the parents, is their doubt of the adequacy of the handicapped to organise their life in any satisfactory or productive way, particularly if they have lived in any form of institution for some time, where everything has been organised and arranged for them. It is felt that too much is being attempted too soon. Parents also have an inner anxiety that if such a placement breaks down, and the hospital or institutional bed is no longer available, then the handicapped person may be returned to their family. For the family this is a double cause of anxiety; firstly, the parents often feel that they will be unable to cope again with all the physical, financial and emotional demands entailed, and secondly it reactivates the permanent dread of 'What will happen when I die?'

*Hostels and residential homes*

These again can be run either by local authorities or by voluntary organisations. These types of accommodation are always staffed and have the great advantage of providing better living facilities than any hospital ever can. Frequently the people living in them go to the nearest social training workshop, so their life is orderly and organised. The problem is, as with so much else, that there are not nearly enough of them to supply the need. In consequence many of those that do exist have long waiting-lists.

*Adult foster homes*

This is a solution for the few who are suitable for such provision, and where the local authorities have the resources to fund it. It is a happy solution where it works but it is, of course, subject to all the strains and precariousness of ordinary fostering. It is also unlikely to be a permanent solution, but it may very well be a useful preparation for a subsequent placement in a group home or hostel.

*Hospitals and hospital units*

Although it has been official policy for over fifteen years to decrease the number of long-stay hospital beds and to increase the community-based services accordingly, it is nevertheless still the case that there are over 40,000 mentally handicapped people resident in mental hospitals. It was never the intention to close all the long-stay hospitals in the foreseeable future, but, as the government DHSS white paper *Care in the Community* made clear in 1981, it was intended at that stage to transfer approximately one-third of the existing residents into community-based alternatives.[10]

The Campaign for Mentally Handicapped People felt in 1986 that it was important, in view of the confused and sometimes alarming reporting, to establish the facts of what had actually happened and produced a report accordingly.[11] The number of residents did, in fact, show a steady decrease, but on the other hand new admissions had sharply increased. Two factors account for these apparently irreconcilable facts: (1) the decrease in numbers has been largely due to the deaths of older long-stay residents, while (2) the increase is mainly due to the increasing use of hospital facilities for short-stay admissions, two-thirds of which are for 'social reasons'. The investigation made clear that most of the closures which had taken place in hospitals and hospital units did not result in the residents being placed in community-based services, for the majority were merely transferred from one institution to another.

On the whole the move appeared to be hampered in that the units that were closed had very inappropriate facilities. Nevertheless the impression is that while the hospitals were rationalising their services not nearly enough effort was being made to find appropriate community-based services. Great improvements have been made, and are being made, to improve the way of life provided in the long-stay hospitals. Much of the credit for this and for the total rethinking of what is appropriate is due to the work of the National Development Group for the Mentally Handicapped.[12] This group was set up in 1975 by the then Secretary of State for Social Services, Barbara Castle, to advise her on mental handicap policy and on its implementation. The winding up of the group was announced in December 1979 by the then secretary of state, Patrick Jenkin, who felt that the group had produced a series of valuable reports but that its closure was appropriate to allow the 'authorities time to absorb and respond to the advice in light of local conditions'.

In relation to the hospitals, one of the most valuable of the group's productions was a check-list detailing all the many social attributes, abilities and activities that hospital staff should be working to establish in the patients in their care. This check-list is comprehensive and very thorough; its only draw-back is that it is so long and time-consuming that it is rarely used in its entirety. Nevertheless, it has had a great influence on current thought and practices.

The long-stay hospitals, despite all the problems imposed by their unsuitable buildings, and even their working practices, which are still largely based on hospital rather than home-making principles, are nevertheless no longer the totally unsatisfactory institutions that were so rightly condemned and rejected. But it is still the permanent dread of some of the parents of both the mentally and the multiply handicapped that this will be the only provision available for their children when they can no longer be contained at home. Some reject the idea so fiercely that they even say, 'Please God we have the courage to commit infanticide, or that we all die in the same accident.' Reactions range from that extreme to the many who fear that hospitalisation will happen but cannot think it is right for their child – for example, the parents in the survey who wrote:

> If we were to die soon, our son would be taken into a subnormality hospital. We can't bear the thought of that, as the set-up of a hospital could never resemble a 'home life' which he is used to, and he would be completely lost. This is not a criticism of the staff in the hospital, but of the system they operate under.

Even those who accept realistically that independent life is not possible for their child make the same point: 'I hate to think she will need to go into a hospital with no individuality of her own.'

At the other extreme, though, there is no doubt that a great number of parents whose children are residents of long-stay hospitals dread the idea of the possible closure of the hospital and the consequent total disruption of their and their children's lives which would follow. So much so that in 1985 an organisation known as RESCARE (the National Society for Mentally Handicapped People in Residential Care) was set up and rapidly attracted a large membership. RESCARE's main plea was that the whole policy should be given more consideration. Some of this reaction may be the result of the increased number of parents who are making use of short-stay relief admissions to the hospitals. This is purely speculative, but it may well be the case that the knowledge of what actually happens when a child or young person is resident in hospital counterbalances the fears that were aroused when all the parents previously knew of such a placement was based on the sensational and often adverse reports which are frequently given more publicity than favourable ones.

It seems clear that slow progress towards community-based alternatives is taking place. But there is also a case for giving much more consideration to its appropriateness for many handicapped people, while at the same time continuing to improve in every way possible the quality of life that can be provided in long-stay institutions.

**The Parents' Choice**

Considering the replies of the parents in the survey to the question of what will happen to their child when they can no longer look after him or her there is no doubt whatever that this is the question which never leaves their minds. The fortunate few have already found their answer: 'Her placement is as permanent as possible in a hostel for the handicapped. She is happy because for the first time in her life these last six years have been spent in a place where people are able to communicate with her in signs.'

There is an important principle exemplified in this reply, namely that it is vitally necessary that the placement is appropriate to needs, and not based on theories of what is desirable. Taking it to an extreme, it would seem probable that if the prime need – in the case above, of being able to communicate – is met, the rest is relatively unimportant. This is very much in line with the recommendations of the CMH report previously mentioned, *Hospital Closures in the Eighties*, which stresses that closures of hospitals and hospital units should take place only when residents are being moved to more favourable and appropriate accommodation based on an 'individual care plan'.

Basically most of the parents' wishes were very simple:

> We would like for him as active and full a life as possible; for him to be able to use his abilities to the full and for a greater understanding of his needs.
>
> We would like to see more homes built for a small 'family' so that the residents, our children, can have all the love and affection they are used to.
>
> We do not like big institutions at all, they are 'cold', and that to us is a place where they can deteriorate and become like vegetables. We do not want that for our son.

> At the moment there appears to be no alternative to a large subnormality hospital. My daughter is not suited to the current trend of hostel living within the community, but she is ideally suited to the more sheltered, family life of a small village-style community.

Another parent whose child was at present in a Steiner school hoped that

> when he reaches school-leaving age he will be able to join one of the Camphill communities and therefore be looked after for the rest of his life. . . . We just hope that the residential care he receives after school-leaving age is as happy and successful as the care he is receiving at present.

The 'day-dream' of another mother for her son was, 'when we are not around to care for him . . . a structured community, with the residents living in a home-like atmosphere caring for themselves and their surroundings as much as possible. There are a few of such places existing, but there are not nearly enough of them.'

An example of the methodical care some parents put into trying to solve the problem was the following excellent summing-up of the whole position as one couple found it:

> This is our greatest problem, and we have been exploring various possibilities in the past seven to eight years. We have looked at Home Farm Trust, Rudolf Steiner schools, local schemes and the MENCAP Houses Foundation. Of these:
>
> (1) The Home Farm Trust seems to provide the optimum solution, with a guarantee of life-long provision *once the child is accepted*. The sting is in the tail, as there is no guarantee of acceptance or of a place becoming available.
> (2) The Rudolf Steiner schools seem to be very good, but we are more than a little concerned about the narrow views which apparently have to be accepted and the imposition of a life-style (e.g. in regard to such things as television) which seem to be very restrictive.
> (3) The MENCAP Houses Foundation scheme appears to provide a solution for 'living in the community', but again there is a provision for 'rejection' of the child *at any time* if she does not prove suitable to the home.
> (4) Local schemes, while providing for accommodation needs, rely heavily on protected workshop conditions to 'pass the time away', which seems to provide an unsuitable life-style.
>
> So we have *no foreseeable solution* to this problem whatever financial obligation we are prepared to undertake.

Taking all the answers together, the parents' choice is undoubtedly for village-style communities where the inmates live in houses and have a sheltered but active life in a caring, home-like atmosphere. The Home Farm Trust and the Steiner communities which both provide this in different ways have already been mentioned. There are others, although, as one mother has said, 'not nearly enough of them'.

An excellent example of these villages are the CARE villages founded by the late Peter Forbes (who was earlier involved in the Home Farm Trust), a man of compassion and true vision whose philosophy was summed up as follows: 'People with . . . handicaps deserve surroundings of quality. If they have been used to it they are entitled to it; if they haven't been used to it then they are even more entitled to it.' The villages he founded carry out this philosophy to the full. There are now six, sited in various parts of the country, and all providing as he planned, an environment which gives the mainly mentally handicapped adults who live in them a dignified but exciting way of life which offers them fulfilment in all ways. The nucleus of the village is a viable farm or nursery garden. Around the main building are the houses in which the villagers live, each with their own room, in family-sized groups. Some of the houses are actually built by the villagers; at the original village in Devon they even made the bricks. These houses are comfortably furnished, and in their own bedroom each villager can surround him- or herself with cherished possessions.

Every villager has a role to play, working either on the farm or in one of the various workshops which are also on the site, producing goods to a standard which makes them saleable in their own right and not as a charitable exercise. Those who are not able to work in any other way are called 'junior house staff' and work in the house or gardens under supervision, to their capacity. Those who work on the farms are trained in husbandry and learn to prepare their stock for the market, and then take it there and sell it at the appropriate time. Every villager has a positive and practical role to play and so rightly feels that they are both contributing to, and needed by, the community. They also know that they are genuinely working, as they all earn wages!

After work they have a varied social life, but – and this is one of the best aspects of the CARE villages – this social life is not exclusively lived in the village, for 'It is no part of CARE philosophy to provide a sheltered life for any of its villagers. The aim has always been to make CARE part of the local community.' This they undoubtedly succeed in doing. A simple example of this is the fact that at Blackerton in Devon they run regular stalls in the market and enter a team in the darts league of the local pub.

It is no wonder that this village way of life is the one preferred by so many parents for their handicapped children. The contrast between the life they provide and that found in even the best of institutions is remarkable. Also, it has now been proved that this way of life can be achieved by the majority of those needing some form of 'sheltered' care. Many of the CARE villagers have moved to the village from hospitals or some other form of institution, and on admission they very often have extremely limited vocabularies, poor if any social skills and a great lack of independence and initiative. The effect of living in the village is dramatic and beneficial in every way. The tragedy is that, although in ordinary terms the growth of the CARE villages has been phenomenal, they can still cater for only a small proportion of those who wish to use them and whose life would be transformed if it were possible for them to do so.

## Notes

1. Warnock Report brief guide, *Meeting Special Educational Needs*, Department of Education and Science, 1978, p. 8.
2. Warnock Report brief guide, as above, p. 10.
3. National Union of Teachers, *Survey of Educational Provision for 16–19-Year-Olds with Special Needs*, London, NUT, 1982.
4. National Bureau for Handicapped Students, unpublished survey, London, 1983.
5. Judy Bradley and Seamus Hegarty, *Students with Special Needs in Further Education*, Progress Report 12, London, Further Education Curriculum Review and Development Unit, 1981, reprinted 1983, 1984.
6. Judy Bradley and Seamus Hegarty, *Stretching the System: A Special Needs Document*, London, Further Education Curriculum Review and Development Unit, 1982.
7. Winifred Tumin, *IYC Trust Notebook for School-Leavers with Special Needs*, London, National Children's Bureau for IYC Trust, 1985.
8. National Development Group for the Mentally Handicapped, *Helping Mentally Handicapped School-Leavers*, Pamphlet No. 3, 1977, reprinted 1981.
9. Warnock Report, brief guide, as above, note 1, p. 10.
10. Department of Health and Social Security, *Care in the Community*, London, HMSO, 1981.
11. Alison Wertheimer, *Hospital Closures in the Eighties*, London, CMH (Campaign for Mentally Handicapped People), 1986.
12. DHSS, *Improving the Quality of Services for Mentally Handicapped People*, A Checklist of Standards, London, National Development Group, 1980.

CHAPTER 7

# Summing Up

## Parents Talking

Until the plight of mentally handicapped people is solved and the outlook becomes brighter for them, parents will find it very difficult to come to terms with the fact that they have a mentally handicapped child. The child does not change before and after you're told it is mentally handicapped, but the outlook on the child's life immediately takes a nose-dive, as the future is so bleak. When are mentally handicapped people going to become an accepted part of the community, like the blind, deaf, dumb and crippled, who can lead fulfilling and rewarding lives within the community? The fate of so many mentally handicapped people is to be placed in an institution where society can forget them, and they are left to vegetate. They deserve more!

Parents also deserve more! The constant stress, which often goes unalleviated for years, causes family break-ups and tension for siblings. *We need help*. A caring environment where we can leave our handicapped child for long or short-term care, and for short periods become a 'normal family', would help. Also some sort of vague assurance that there will be a place somewhere for our child after school-leaving age, where he can live his life with dignity, would give us some peace of mind.

The reality of having to cope and of having a handicapped child takes a while to adjust to. . . . It is all such an unknown quantity.

I probably sound bitter and sorry for myself. I *am* bitter. I feel sickened by the attitude of the majority of people to the handicapped and their families. I am *not* sorry for myself, just sad and very worried.

Getting equipment is very difficult, so often it gets overlooked by the DHSS, or they can't afford it. This is on such things as potty aids, walking frames, bath aids, even wheel chairs: normal *everyday* needs. It means endless phone calls, demands, and then sometimes you have to go to a charity.

I don't know one parent of a handicapped child who doesn't feel guilty about having one, and when you see that people who are disabled by industrial accident or war are awarded far higher government grants and benefits than those unfortunate enough to be disabled at birth, it reinforces the idea that somehow it was your fault. It is hard to say how it all affects you, save that it is probably the worst thing that can happen to anyone - the one thing that stays with you always. The pain never diminishes. As the child grows, the handicap becomes more obvious and affects the whole family more. You have to be very tough.

As this is a book for parents of special children, the word that hit me straight between the eyes was 'understanding' - that's all *I* was looking for.

The most we wish is for him to be happy. It has been accepted now - but only over the last year or so - that what makes his happiness and satisfaction is not what constitutes ours. It is all a gradual acceptance of a situation. His life will be different, but we are in no position to judge it. He is very special to us, with special problems, but so is our daughter, and we wish them both well. He, however, has altered our lives to such an extent that it is difficult to get into words. One feels that he will be a source of enrichment for us for as long as we can appreciate it.

## Acceptance and Understanding

In this book the attempt has been made to look at the consequences of having a handicapped child through the eyes of the parents, and also to discover what resources are available to help them. It is a very difficult task to undertake, since, as one parent rightly pointed out, no one who is not in such a position can truly appreciate what it is like. This is why, wherever possible and where appropriate, parents' actual words have been used. There is a further difficulty in that the fact of having a handicapped child of one kind or another does not turn the parents into a homogeneous group. In fact, it has clearly emerged how frequently parents get the feeling that they are regarded as such, and that to the world at large they have ceased to be individuals and are just regarded as 'handicapped parents'. This is both damaging and hurtful and something that we can all do something about. Perhaps all that it needs initially is a change of emphasis, so that we do truly look on the child first as a *child* and then consider the rest. Two key words keep coming to mind, and they are *acceptance* and *understanding*.

To be of real use, acceptance and understanding should operate right from the moment that the fact of handicap is established. It has been shown that many improvements are needed in the way parents are first given the news that they have a 'special' child. Fortunately, in today's economic climate, this is something that need not cost money to improve. The professional training of doctors is beginning to be modified so that they are now made much more aware of the need to consider the emotional reactions of their patients as well as their physical needs. Giving bad news is never an easy task, but it is possible to teach the necessary understanding which will make it easier for all concerned, and this is now starting to happen.

However, too much should not be demanded of the doctors. They should be able to rely with confidence on being supported in caring for this side of the parents' needs, once they have fulfilled their professional responsibility of diagnosing, and then communicating the news, and have given the parents as much information as possible at this stage of the consequences of the handicap plus some guidance as to how to deal with it. One possibility would seem to be to use the other professionals who are normally involved, i.e. health visitors or social workers. The problem is that these workers do not have sufficient time to give parents the constant support they usually need at this stage; their case-load is too heavy. Nevertheless, there are some who are particularly interested in this part of their professional task and who do somehow find the time to do it. In the case of the mentally handicapped, community nurses, where they exist, do admirable work in this respect.

Warnock recognised the need for this service and put forward the concept of the 'named person' as a means of meeting it. The 'named person' would be notified to the parents as the one they could turn to when in need of advice or information. Unfortunately the suggestion was not included in the statutory legislation but was left to local authorities to implement as they chose. This has meant, once again, that there is a great discrepancy in the way it is carried out.

Many of the parents in the survey indicated that they would welcome most the intervention of another parent whose child had a similar handicap to that of their child. They felt that they would gain a great deal from being able to share their reactions, problems and experiences. As has been discussed earlier (Chapter 2), many parents have themselves initiated ways in which this can be done, and the account given of the work done by the Southend Group and other similar bodies shows how successfully this can be organised. However, this should not be the only option, since it relies on a body of people being available who not only can establish working co-operation with the professionals involved but are also competent and knowedgeable enough to meet parents' needs, and also to train other parents in the task. Further, much though parents appreciate this kind of help, they do not all want to do it in their turn. Nor do they want to find that, because they are trying to do it, while at the same time coping with the extra demands they have to meet in caring for their own handicapped child, they have no time or opportunity for any other kind of social activity. No one would want to prevent the parents who are willing and able to undertake the task from doing so, but alternatives should be available, to ensure that such help can always be given to those parents who feel that they would benefit from it.

There might be a case for setting up such a service more formally and enlisting the help of other interested people, as for instance those who have a handicapped sibling, or the mothers of normal children whose offspring are able to care for themselves to a large extent. As mothers, they would have shared many of the experiences of the mothers of the handicapped. Also, if it can be assumed that one way to change attitudes is to emphasise the needs of the handicapped child, first as a child, then it would seem to be a logical extension of this to emphasise the shared experience of 'mothering' common to the mothers of the 'normal' and the handicapped. A further advantage would be that many more people were gaining a realistic knowledge of handicap. This might well result in reducing some of the superstitions, fears and tensions associated with handicap which still linger in many people's minds, even if they are largely unrecognised and unacknowledged.

The fact that volunteers are always found when, for instance, a respite care service is being initiated indicates that they would be available for this service also. It would be an advantage for such a service, if it were started, to be formalised to some extent, and for some form of training to be offered to the volunteers. This would give the necessary information they would need to deal with parents' factual questions and also give them the security of being part of a recognised service. The training would not need to be too extensive, because the main role of these volunteers would simply be to provide the acceptance and the 'listening ear' that so many parents feel they lack. Health visitors, social workers and community nurses could all be involved in making the introductions and could also be referred to when professional knowledge was required. Finally, this would help parents avoid the feeling of being 'trapped', as so many now feel they are, in a 'circle of handicap' in which they meet only others who have the same problems as they have themselves.

As has already been stated, one of the main purposes of this book has been to describe some of the problems faced by parents, and then to give examples of good solutions to them, many of which have been devised in the first place by the parents themselves. It should be emphasised again that there are other good examples besides those that have been described; these have been omitted simply because there has not been room to include them all. What is very frustrating, however, is that they tend to exist in isolation, and that the good examples set have not been taken up and developed by those who should have been in a position to do this. Where services have been started, their development has depended totally on there being someone with the motivation and drive to begin the process.

Honeylands in Exeter is a first-class example of this. Started by Professor Brindlecombe when he was a medical officer of health, based on what he had established to be what parents of handicapped children wanted and needed, this very valuable service was set up as part of a general paediatric service. If it can be done in East Devon, why cannot similar units be part of paediatric services all over the country? Parents do not complain or appear to resent the fact that the main task of setting up services seems to fall to them, but it is surely wrong that this should be the case. Perhaps they *should* complain more!

In another area a group of parents who had visited Honeylands described it as their 'dream come true' and wished that there was a Honeylands in their area. They even asked a group of visiting officials why there was not. They were 'fobbed off' with the answer that, good as it was, it was not the only way to provide such services and that they should all be looked at before any were set up. A marvellous rationalisation? Needless to say, there is no evidence that anything has materialised; presumably they are still looking. Meanwhile, the parents continue to struggle to provide what they can from their own resources. 'From the existing resources': these words haunt all advances in all areas. Official approval is freely given to many good schemes, but not the money needed to set them up.

It would be unfair to be too condemnatory, however. Many advances and improvements have been made. In the field of education there have been great developments and allied to this is the growth of such schemes as Portage (see Chapter 4). Some criticisms have been made of this scheme, but there is no denying that it has been instrumental in bringing a new approach to the help that can be given to the handicapped child and parents, almost from birth. Portage has also provoked new thinking among those who criticise it as to better alternatives. Another great improvement has been the advancing of the school admission age, enabling children with special needs to go to school from the age of two.

There seems little doubt that for the parents of these children the school years are, on the whole, the easiest time. This is in spite of the fact that the present time is one of educational change, and there are many conflicting views on aspects of the new design. Parents are still very divided as to whether all the changes will be to their children's advantage. Some welcome them, while others wonder if they will lose some of the things they have come to value highly if their child is transferred into the mainstream school. They would possibly not be so worried if they were assured that 'parental choice' really did operate as it was intended to in all areas. But evidence has shown that it does not. It is still the complaint of many parents that they had no choice; and, even if they appear to have one, if their views for their child do not coincide with the authorities' decision they can be overruled.

The report produced by the Spastics Society, *Caught in the Act* (see Chapter 5), illuminated another cause for complaint, showing how few local education authorities carried out their responsibility of informing parents of assessment procedures and of their legal right to be fully consulted. On the other hand, the example set by Derbyshire has shown how true partnership can be achieved if the authority wishes for it. Hopefully, many of the problems are those of early days of a changing situation. When more time has passed, allowing for proper assessment of the value of the changes to be made, then will be the time to make decisions. It is to be hoped that at that time no one – parents or professionals – will overlook the need to ask the very basic question, 'Are the changes doing all that was hoped to improve the position of handicapped children?' Included in this discussion when it does take place should be the children themselves, many of whom will have opinions that they will be able to express.

There is one aspect of these years which is still not fully considered and that is the problem of the time when the children are not in school. Throughout the year there is a need for out-of-school recreational and social activities. The MENCAP Gateway Clubs go some way towards fulfilling the need for some of the handicapped, but many parents wish that more clubs and organisations such as the Scouts and Guides could more frequently include and involve the handicapped as part of their normal activity, not simply as objects for charitable exercises.

The problem of school holidays is also one where more relief is needed. Very often the long summer holiday reduces the family nearly to breaking point. Here again there are some reasonable options, though not nearly enough; and if no sort of funding is provided those that are available are often too expensive for a family to afford. This is why, often through sheer need of some sort of relief, parents have to accept the cheapest rather than the most suitable form of relief. Societies such as Dr Barnardo's and the Church of England Children's Society do as much as they can, but often a short-stay placement in a hostel or hospital for the mentally handicapped is all that is available. These are hardly the places one would choose for a holiday.

The area where least has been achieved is also the one that causes parents the most anxiety, and that is the post-school life of their children. With proper education and suitable facilities for self-help and self-care there are some handicapped people who can live an independent life in the community, but this is not the case for the majority; yet the greater the need for provision the less that is acceptable is available. It is here that 'community care' becomes a cruel farce and can impose an intolerable burden on parents or other care-givers who have already worked for years to try to help and improve their handicapped family member. It cannot be emphasised too strongly how difficult and unpleasant in many ways such a task can be. To state but one aspect of it, even the task of cleaning up an incontinent child becomes less pleasant as the child becomes older and bigger; how much worse it is therefore when this service has to be given day in and day out, year by year, with little hope of relief, to an incontinent adult, especially perhaps when the carer and the cared-for are linked by emotional and familial ties. At the same time, the financial situation of the family may be deteriorating because of the need for someone to be available to give this care. A bad situation becomes worse when, as is not unknown, parents are not informed of the assistance and relief they could be given. There is no excuse for this, no matter how busy the professionals are.

The natural course of events is for children to grow up and leave the parental home to set up their own. This is an outcome that the parents of the handicapped cannot count upon. Even some who do achieve it only do so either by means of a long and often bitter battle with the authorities or by being compelled to settle for a way of life they would never have chosen for their children. Credit should be given to the great improvements that are being made, sometimes in the most unrewarding conditions, in the mental hospitals. Very often the criticisms that are still correctly made arise from lack of resources and gross understaffing.

There are always a certain number of the handicapped who genuinely need the kind of care that can be provided only in a medical setting. What is unacceptable to parents and to many besides is the number who do ultimately go to live in hospitals because there is no alternative available. As the report *Hospital Closures in the Eighties* has revealed (see Chapter 6), the reports of hospital closures and patient transfer too often conceal the fact that patients are merely being moved from one institution to another and are no better off in consequence. In the area studied this applied to 68 per cent of the former residents, while only 17 per cent had moved into hostels or community units. The same report made the rather surprising disclosure that, although central government had made welfare benefits available to purchase better accommodation in the private or voluntary sector, at the time of the report very little use had been made of this type of provision by the health authorities. There is a great deal to be done at this end of the service.

The overall picture is that in every area there are some reasonable or good facilities to be found, but there are not nearly enough of them. This applies in the field of further education as much as to the residential provision. It is difficult to determine why this is so. Every good facility that is provided is immediately used to the full. Good and successful models have been set up showing what can be done for very seriously afflicted people such as the deaf/blind, or in providing a rewarding and fulfilling way of life as in the village communities. Once established, these communities are often less expensive to run than the institutions, particularly when (as is often the case) the skills acquired by the residents can contribute to reducing the costs.

One possible but purely speculative answer could be that there are too many agencies involved, and that each of these agencies has to care for many services. This means that the apparently less pressing needs are frequently overlooked. Further delays occur when responsibility has to be transferred from one service to another, and with the limited resources that are available impossible choices are often imposed. One such that comes to mind is the need to choose between providing sorely needed speech therapy for language-disordered children and an extra machine for kidney patients needing dialysis (a true example). On what possible grounds can such a choice be made? A case could well be made for reconsidering and possibly redistributing responsibilities to provide a more efficient, and possibly less expensive, service than exists at present.

Going back to the question posed at the beginning of this book – does the community do all that it can to help the parents with their unsought dilemma? – it is very difficult to give an unqualified answer. Many improvements have been and are being made. There is much more public awareness of the need, and many good models have been set up. More financial support is available. But in spite of all these things it is impossible to claim that all the services and resources which are needed are freely available in every part of the country.

Too much still seems to depend on where people happen to live and on the inclinations and choices of those in power in that area. Even the best-disposed authorities are limited in what they can do by the resources which are available to them. There is even a doubt in some minds as to whether the changes that are being made are always in the best interests of the people they are claimed to help. The most cynical even question whether 'community care' and 'integration' are not rationalisations whose greatest contribution is limited at reducing costs rather than effecting real improvements. A case could certainly be made in some instances for feeling that too many of these 'improvements' are based on theory rather than on experimentally proved facts.

Improvements seem slow when one is personally involved in a tragic situation, but it is obviously impossible to make fundamental wide-reaching changes, such as the closure of many hospitals, in a short space of time. A valid criticism, however, is the slow rate of implementing many of the statutory changes, such as the legal obligation of the local authorities to give full information about procedures to the parents of children with special needs. Another is the great lack of proper facilities for those most severely afflicted, especially perhaps the multiply handicapped. It appears to be true that, unless pressure is persisted in, improvements will not be made; it must never be assumed that the fact that legislation has been passed automatically means that it will be implemented.

There is one basic and major improvement which can be made which requires no legislation or increase in resources but would probably bring about the greatest possible change in the lives of those families who have a handicapped member. That is for everyone to accept the fact of handicap in such a way that those who have to suffer the pain of having it in their family do not have to dread the reactions of others, coming to feel that they must either retreat from all contacts or fight to be recognised and accepted and to have their needs appreciated. As one mother said: 'After you have learnt the news that your child is handicapped, the child is still the same as he was before. All that alters is the way everyone regards him and you also.'

The child is still a child, with a child's needs for love and acceptance; the parents are still the people they were before, but in need of acceptance and understanding. They are very vulnerable and can be easily hurt by insensitive behaviour. A cruel example of this is the case of the relatives who sent presents to all the other children in a family but never sent anything to the handicapped child. Another, not intended to be hurtful but felt deeply by the mother, was the case of the school which at Christmas-time gave all the children presents appropriate to their age, but a toy intended for a toddler to the child in the group with special needs.

Allied to this is the wish of the parents to be *listened* to, especially by the professionals. They would be prepared to accept that they were wrong if their views were discussed and taken seriously. What they find intolerable is to have them dismissed as the 'fussy behaviour of an over-anxious mother' or to have them brushed aside as not being worthy of consideration.

Francis Bacon in his essay 'Of Parents and Children' says: 'Children sweeten labour but they make misfortune more bitter.' These words can be applied to the parents of children with special needs, although not precisely in their original meaning. For to these parents, the sweetness, the labour and the misfortune all stem from the child. In the same essay Bacon also says: 'The joys of parents are secret and so are their griefs and fears.' To a large extent this secrecy and privacy is one of the many things these parents miss; their life is inevitably invaded and laid open by the needs of their child.

It seems appropriate that the last words in this book should come from the parents themselves, so they will follow and end this account.

> I feel that these children, when born, are, as we all know, very special. And although they take up so much of your time, much more than other children, caring for them seems much more rewarding.
>
> Bringing up a handicapped child is totally different from bringing up able-bodied children. You have to look for different achievements – learning to swallow, to look, to hold her head up, to sit on a box.
>
> I don't see my daughter as a problem. Problems are created by other people.
>
> The help that you get or even get offered is very much dependent on whom you have dealings with.
>
> I would have liked people to recognise my child's potential and listen to me, and I deeply resented having my child referred to as a 'case study'.
>
> My little girl is loved, and she loves us. She brings out the best in everyone who meets her, so I am told. She is a constant joy to us all and she has made us view life from a totally different angle.
>
> Reading all this, it seems a very sad, hard life, but it isn't. The joy, love and friendships outnumber all the problems.
>
> It has been very frustrating at times coping with a feeling that 'specialists' think that parents are difficult, troublesome, even arrogant, when all they want is answers and a bit of help and encouragement.
>
> We just want to be treated and listened to as normal people, not as handicapped people.

And finally, the hope for the future:

> We would like to think that society would have learned really to care about the less fortunate.

# Index